The ... *ê*

D1428622

The Humanities and Everyday Life

The Literary Agenda

The Humanities and Everyday Life

MICHAEL LEVENSON

OXFORD
UNIVERSITY PRESS

OXFORD
UNIVERSITY PRESS

Great Clarendon Street, Oxford, OX2 6DP,
United Kingdom

Oxford University Press is a department of the University of Oxford.
It furthers the University's objective of excellence in research, scholarship,
and education by publishing worldwide. Oxford is a registered trade mark of
Oxford University Press in the UK and in certain other countries

Published in the United States of America by Oxford University Press
198 Madison Avenue, New York, NY 10016, United States of America

British Library Cataloguing in Publication Data
Data available

Library of Congress Control Number: 2017941742

ISBN 978-0-19-880829-9

Printed in Great Britain by
Clays Ltd, St Ives plc

Series Introduction

The Crisis in, the Threat to, the Plight of the Humanities: enter these phrases in Google's search engine and there are 23 million results, in a great fifty-year-long cry of distress, outrage, fear, and melancholy. Grant, even, that every single anxiety and complaint in that catalogue of woe is fully justified—the lack of public support for the arts, the cutbacks in government funding for the humanities, the imminent transformation of a literary and verbal culture by visual/virtual/digital media, the decline of reading... And still, though it were all true, and just because it might be, there would remain the problem of the response itself. Too often there's recourse to the shrill moan of offended piety or a defeatist withdrawal into professionalism.

The Literary Agenda is a series of short polemical monographs that believes there is a great deal that needs to be said about the state of literary education inside schools and universities and more fundamentally about the importance of literature and of reading in the wider world. The category of 'the literary' has always been contentious. What *is* clear, however, is how increasingly it is dismissed or is unrecognized as a way of thinking or an arena for thought. It is sceptically challenged from within, for example, by the sometimes rival claims of cultural history, contextualized explanation, or media studies. It is shaken from without by even greater pressures: by economic exigency and the severe social attitudes that can follow from it; by technological change that may leave the traditional forms of serious human communication looking merely antiquated. For just these reasons this is the right time for renewal, to start reinvigorated work into the meaning and value of literary reading for the sake of the future.

It is certainly no time to retreat within institutional walls. For all the academic resistance to 'instrumentalism', to governmental measurements of public impact and practical utility, literature exists in and across society. The 'literary' is not pure or specialized or self-confined; it is not restricted to the practitioner in writing or the academic in studying. It exists in the whole range of the world which is its subject matter: it consists in what non-writers actively receive from writings when, for example, they start to see the world more imaginatively as a result of reading novels and begin to think more carefully about human personality. It comes from literature making available much of human life that would not otherwise be existent to thought or recognizable as knowledge. If it is true that involvement in literature, so far from being a minority aesthetic, represents a significant contribution to the life of human thought, then that idea has to be argued at the public level without succumbing to a hollow rhetoric or bowing to a reductive world view. Hence the effort of this series to take its place *between* literature and the world. The double-sided commitment to occupying that place and establishing its reality is the only 'agenda' here, without further prescription as to what should then be thought or done within it.

What is at stake is not simply some defensive or apologetic 'justification' in the abstract. The case as to why literature matters in the world not only has to be argued conceptually and strongly tested by thought: it should be given presence, performed, and brought to life in the way that literature itself does. That is why this series includes the writers themselves, the novelists and poets, in order to try to close the gap between the thinking of the artists and the thinking of those who read and study them. It is why it also involves other kinds of thinkers—the philosopher, the theologian, the psychologist, the neuroscientist— examining the role of literature within their own life's work and thought, and the effect of that work, in turn, upon literary thinking. This series admits and encourages personal voices in an unpredictable variety of individual approach and expression, speaking wherever possible across countries and disciplines and temperaments. It aims for something more than intellectual assent: rather, the literary sense of what it is like to feel the thought, to embody an idea in a person, to bring it to being in a narrative or in aid of adventurous reflection. If the artists refer to their own works, if other thinkers return to ideas that have marked much of their working life, that is not their vanity nor a failure of originality. It is what the series has asked of them: to speak out of what they know and care about, in whatever language can best serve their most serious thinking, and without the necessity of trying to cover every issue or meet every objection in each volume.

Philip Davis

Contents

Contents

Introduction

This short book offers a reading of the place and prospects of the humanities at the present moment, nearly two decades into the new millennium. It asks us to locate humanistic study within the wide field of everyday life and to consider how academic practices intersect with the aims and habits of those outside university walls. At the same time, it looks toward "ordinary life" within the academy, the everyday conduct of research, teaching, ranking, and mentorship within the scholarly workspace.

We regularly think of "the humanities" as comprising a cluster of specialized and university-based activities, whose values depend upon internal coherence and separation from the undisciplined exchange of ideas. The separation is at once physical and intellectual. Professional researchers and teachers occupy the quiet enclaves of libraries, archives, small offices, and common rooms; they exchange ideas with students and one another in conferences, colloquia, and classrooms; they publish books and articles with modest circulation. The success of these arrangements, as well as the controversies they have recently stirred, can obscure broader and smaller doings. In light of this thought, the present book engages with the shared space of the lecture hall and the seminar room, and the cross-generational complexities of academic exchange; it considers the architecture of universities as the material and symbolic setting for the ordinary course of academic work; it asks questions of credentials and hierarchy, and the efforts to assess performance through quantitative measure. The humanities move uneasily but productively between lonely individual thought, local community, and encompassing world. Throughout, the book regards academic life as a social formation often unconscious of its historical condition and the implications of its full collective character.

Beyond the precincts of the university, with or without degrees, people ponder meanings at home, in their offices, or in public spaces. They pursue research into cherished subjects—local history, quilts, antique cars, detective fiction (to take examples only from my own family)—and they establish their own terms of conversation, their norms of agreement and disagreement. Well beyond the university, people devise commentaries and theories about texts they read and music they hear, and also about the direction of the modern world and the basis for moral value. These are ongoing subjects of everyday humanities. One emphasis of the book falls upon the recovery of these daily practices in their variety, durability, and close texture. Examples include the activities of book clubs, museum-goers, private collectors, domestic genealogists, historical re-enactors, editors of *Wikipedia*.

Preservative, Comparative, Interpretative, Self-Interrogative—I take these activities as the coordinates of research and teaching in the academic humanities, but also as conditions of our everyday encounters with chosen artifacts. Like their academic counterparts, ordinary humanists recover what has been lost, overlooked or ill-tended; they interpret the obscurities in the texts and objects they gather; in a globalizing world, they compare national exempla to one another, and, in endlessly modernizing times, they set the cultural past against its present. As ample testimony confirms, these everyday practitioners examine themselves and their historical moment as they proceed, interrogating assumptions, methods, and values.

A more inclusive view shows the convergence and collision of professional and non-professional domains; it also inevitably raises questions concerning professional and amateur. Within this frame, the book offers an account of *expertise*, which has itself become a timely area of research as well as a controversial topic within political life. We need to ask again what constitutes expertise, how it varies in different domains, and what claims it can make for itself. The burden of argument here is that expertise has grown vulnerable because the terms of its identification remain mystified and contestable. The expert witness in a legal trial, the scientific and policy expert, the expert in a scholarly field—all require critique as well as defense. By addressing the question from the standpoint of the humanities, expert and lay perspectives might open to new view.

The Humanities and Everyday Life proposes that we resist the assumption that dispersed knowledge—incomplete, fragmentary, not yet organized, not yet disciplined or expert—is foreign to academic achievement. Part of professorial self-esteem rests on participation in a system of disciplines. But alongside discipline stands the productively un-disciplined character of the university. The architecture of knowledge—physical and intellectual—means that specialists perpetually confront the boundaries of command, credential, and discipline, and find themselves as shy guests, gazing at possible vocations in offices and buildings near at hand. Before colleagues in other areas of thought, they often become, again, curious and tentative. A task for the book, then, is to weigh the effects of such everyday routines on and within the academy, and also, reversing the vector, to recover the disciplines of knowledge within extra-academic lives.

Stefan Collini has recently made bracing and influential claims for the distinctive qualities of universities. They share features with other institutions, says Collini, such as corporate research teams or learned associations. But the university retains some telling marks of difference—for instance, "That it furthers some form of advanced scholarship or research whose character is not wholly dictated by the need to solve immediate practical problems."[1] Collini goes further, emphasizing the singular responsibility of universities to train the staff of the next generation. Not only, that is, do we keep ourselves apart from immediate practice; we educate students to follow us, preparing them to take our places in an ongoing tradition of inquiry. These are important claims within a tenacious argument. Here I mean to complement Collini, by asking, not what distinguishes the humanities and universities from the wider world, but what connects them—what entangles and implicates them. After all, while it is true that we prepare students to become our successors, these make only a small band among those we teach. By far, the greater number move through the university on their way to other work in other spaces. On any given campus around the world, the largest population will be those traversing a few well-remembered years on their way to lives elsewhere—those for whom academic life is means, not end. It may be best to think of this contrast as the more characteristic feature of universities: that they have a deeply mixed character, created by the encounter of those few who claim the autonomy of inquiry and academic vocation with those many others, who frankly and cheerfully accept other-than-academic destinies. We tend to speak as though the struggle is between academic and non-academic parties, forgetting that they meet within the academy itself.

The university is not only a matrix of disciplines, formal research, and teaching curriculum. The paradigm of the curious museum-goer is as important as that of the scholar in the Bodleian. My task in these pages is to locate the daily round of the humanities between those paradigms: between sustained, even lifetime, absorption in a professional field of study and a stroll through a gallery, stirred by first glimpses toward new or half-known subjects. We find ourselves possessing just a piece of the history of Akhenaten; we are intrigued but amateur in the theory of Russian Ego-Cubism; we realize we know all too little about Neoplatonism. Each partial view can suggest a life vocation, as it has for someone else. If we think of everyday life as opposed to the rigors of discipline, we can find ourselves abashed to find the everyday inside, not safely outside, the university.

Nor is the everyday as everyday as it appears. I can press this thought by way of a shrewd interlocutor, namely Joseph Conrad, writer and sailor. At a difficult moment in his career, at a moment when he was losing confidence in his own mastery as a writer, Conrad began a memoir of his sailing career, publishing it in 1905 under the title, *The Mirror of the Sea.* He had worked on shipboard for many years, long before it occurred to him to become a novelist. In his memoir he sets to recover the discipline of life at sea in terms that bear upon our lives on land, and within academic walls. Here is Conrad, insisting on a special language of expertise suitable to seamanship:

> [The chief mate] is the man who watches the growth of the cable—a sailor's phrase which has all the force, precision, and imagery of technical language … created by simple men with keen eyes for the real aspect of the things they see in their trade, … [He asks,] "How does the cable grow?" Because "grow" is the right word for the long drift of a cable emerging aslant under the strain, taut as a bow-string above the water. And it is the voice of the keeper of the ship's anchors that will answer: "Grows right ahead, sir," or "Broad on the bow," or whatever concise and deferential shout will fit the case.[2]

Life at sea, everyday life at sea, acquires a precision, a regimen, and a shared language of its own. It is, Conrad says, a "bread-winning" labor, but it also attracts a value independent of bread:

> [The] skill of technique is more than honesty; it is something wider, embracing honesty and grace and rule in an elevated and clear sentiment, not altogether utilitarian, which may be called the honor of labour. It is made up of accumulated tradition, kept alive by individual pride, rendered exact by professional opinion, and, like the higher arts, it is spurred on and sustained by discriminating praise.[3]

Yes, he will write in *A Personal Record*, there is "criticism at sea," a "quarter-deck criticism," just as there is "literary criticism."[4] I take this picture as a striking example of the workings of a discipline, a discipline in Conrad's words, "not altogether utilitarian." It depends precisely on overcoming what I have described as the dispersal of knowledge: the diffusion of insight, the stray gazing among unknown objects. Conrad is acutely aware of intellectual life ashore—the whole apparatus of text and criticism—but he insists on the coherence and professionalism of work at sea, its technical language, its body of criticism, its life in time, its shared and self-conscious values. Disciplines are not the exclusive property of the academy, just as everyday life is not somehow elsewhere.

They are adjacent activities—professional humanities, folk humanities, literary criticism, quarterdeck criticism—adjacent activities, which have unfolded in near complete mutual disregard. They should interpenetrate and inter-animate. Their work—preservative, interpretive, comparative, self-interrogative—should overstep any border that we are tempted to preserve. We need knowledge as expertise but also knowledge as diffusion and dispersal—knowledge as discipline but also as undisciplined curiosity in a museum. Our task now is not to strengthen walls around the humanities, but to roam widely beneath their banner. More humanities, not more apologies.

*

The first chapter of the book, the "The Humanities at Large," lays out the wide field of activity beyond the university. It begins with Joyce's Bloom passing through the streets of Dublin, keen to understand, but also sharply aware of the constraints on amateur knowledge. Bloom is an archetype of the everyday humanist, but he's not the only one. We know that a growing number of small groups meet over shared enthusiasm for reading, viewing, listening, and thinking in company. They encounter and interpret a broad diversity of texts and artifacts; they trace histories and build geographies; they recover (and often perform) historical events. The chapter presents a series of cases: most decisively the conversations in book clubs, and the contributions to *Wikipedia*, quite different cases, but each a conspicuous example of inquiry beyond the university, each offering a surprising complexity and standing in illuminating contrast to academic practice.

I then turn directly to the daily life of the university, looking to recover the social setting of the academic humanities. This second chapter begins by connecting the tasks of research and the aims of teaching to the specificities of workaday routines: the array of administrative responsibilities, the division of department labor, the chafing irritations of scarce resources, the incidental distractions and unexpected pleasures. Much achievement in the humanities results from solitary effort. But its individual cast should not obscure the social habitats that encourage or obstruct it. The classroom, the department, and the building corridors produce a complex sociology of small groups, including the overlooked community of adjunct instructors and the laboring teams of custodial staff. Then, beyond the university stand powerful systems of evaluation and award. The discussion concludes by recalling the mere activity of thought within the daily dislocations and constraints.

The book's middle chapter gives an account of expertise, which stands at the conceptual pivot of my study. A first contrast distinguishes between the professional legitimation of expertise—by degree, appointment, publication, promotion, and title—and the acceptance of experts through informal acknowledgment and tacit agreement. But each domain generates contrasts and unsettlements of its own. The law has long struggled with the status of expert testimony, generating controversies that have taken a new turn in the nearly quarter-century since the case of *Daubert v. Merrell Dow Pharmaceuticals Inc.* at the United States Supreme Court. During that same period, "science studies" raised theoretical questions about the awarding of expert authority in science and technical policy. As I prepared this text during 2016, controversies over the privilege of experts repeatedly entered political debate, sharply so in the Brexit referendum and the American election campaign, cases which underscore the urgency of the question. As the chapter means to show, the humanities occupy a distinctive place in both the theory and the controversy.

The daily tasks of the humanities must find a place for themselves, at once social and architectural. The concern of the fourth chapter is with the spaces of community within both academic and non-academic domains. Around the globe, a new architecture has come to dominate the construction of cultural spaces. Museums, galleries, public libraries, and university buildings display a striking, convergent, and recent aesthetic, an International Style of academic construction. Such buildings stand alongside older and more humble spaces, which carry their own symbolic force and practical function. The chapter sets exteriors against interiors and the circulation of thought within the physical constraints enjoined by the competing styles of old and new. It places libraries and museums alongside university lecture halls and seminar rooms. The plan is to follow the course of the humanities within the containers that must house it, that enclose and disclose the exchange of knowledge. At every stage, the concern is with the formation of cultural community within these spaces, the stresses upon community, and the efforts to preserve it. The last phase of the chapter thinks about the humanities in relation to religious life.

The last substantial chapter turns from space to time, asking how the humanities live in history and through change. The passage of intellectual generations, the succession of subjects and methods, the problem of mentorship—these are leading concerns here. They stand alongside the practice of amateur genealogy, which, since the appearance of Haley's *Roots* in 1976, and then after the emergence of web-based resources for family history, has become a serious commitment for so many private individuals. Genealogy raises its own new questions for the everyday humanities, questions of motive and method; it also contrasts and intersects with academic history. The disputes between professional historians and zealous amateurs, and the recent rap-prochement between the two groups, cast useful light on relations between private and professional humanists. It also reopens the question of interdisciplinarity, as raising its own problem of affiliation, succession, and family resemblance.

Virginia Woolf places a condition on the guineas that she is willing to contribute to the cause of women's education. She will offer the money happily, but it must be spent toward the making of a new college that declines to accept barriers of separation. Within her historical metaphor, it must be a "poor college," "founded on poverty and youth," teaching "only the arts that can be taught cheaply." Woolf's conceit of 1937 is a prod to contemporary thought. In my conclusion, it gives an occasion for reflecting on what might now be possible for the humanities and the everyday humanities, and how the gifts (and expertise) might run in both directions. Woolf's conceit is at once elegy and a prod to new thought.

A point worth stressing here, and mentioning from time to time in the pages to come, is that the condition of the humanities often resembles the situation of the university as such. "Humanities," "liberal arts," "the university,"—a useful slippage unsteadies the use of these terms. Rather than harden the boundaries around them, the approach here is to move among the words as the argument demands. This is a work about the humanities which hopes also to contribute to thinking about the future of the university.

The book avoids the rhetoric of emergency, as in "the crisis of the humanities." Of course, there are urgent issues for the university and especially its humane disciplines. But the pressing issues are at the same time chronic problems that cannot be resolved in any thinkably near future. Crisis talk becomes thin, brittle, predictable. The enterprise of the humanities will not disappear: the demand to preserve, compare, and interpret is securely embedded in too many people and too many long-standing social practices. So too is a readiness to pose difficult questions, both to the arrangements of the world and to the arrangements of the self. The counter-forces are strong, growing, and better-funded. What's new?

Notes

1. Stefan Collini, *What Are Universities For?* (London: Penguin, 2012), 7.
2. Joseph Conrad, *The Mirror of the Sea* (New York and London: Harper & Brothers, 1906), 31.
3. Ibid., 37.
4. Joseph Conrad, *A Personal Record* (New York and London: Harper & Brothers, 1912), 184.

1

The Humanities at Large

In its faint technical flavor, as in its common use, the term "humanities" evokes images of university settings. But according to any useful working definition, including those used here, the humanities are everywhere. What else do we think we're doing when we collect stamps and coins, gather to discuss books, challenge one another's values, display engravings, debate musical taste, or visit museums? This first chapter and the book's impetus depend on such recognition: that not only our understanding of the humanities, but our hopes for their flourishing future, will depend on acknowledging the humanities in ordinary life.

But there are difficulties. Anyone who works in colleges or universities is likely to recall meeting strangers on the grounds. Tourists, parents, the idly curious find themselves, say, on the edge of an academic green. A gate or wall may obtrude. Students will be walking purposively; they follow a labyrinth of paths. The arrangement of buildings can appear as a diagram of obligations and routines only half-illuminated by the standing maps that indicate "You are here!" The posture of these visitors shows uncertainty. I have overheard couples and trios wondering "if it's all right to be here," or asking, "Can anyone go in?" Even when accompanied by their enrolled children, they hang back cautiously.

Partly, these are signs of deference, partly a sense of mystery or bewilderment. In either case, they express the separation between academic life and the world outside. An ancient whiff of the cloister still hangs over academic doings, even in noisy urban settings. And then, superimposed on the aura of initiation and ritual, is a brisk modern tone of professionalism. Each is forbidding to the outsider. Almost all places in a university can make visitors tentative, the laboratory as much as the seminar room. But the humanities and the humanistic social sciences create a special uneasiness. Where the chemistry lab and the lecture on microeconomics have analogies in the non-academic workplace, the elucidation of poetic form or a discussion of the categorical imperative can appear to belong to a universe, and universe of discourse, all its own.

Particularly when the task is interpretative and contention reaches a crux, the conversation can move dizzily back to assumptions and first principles. The motto, for instance, that all philosophy is Philosophy I, captures the power of origins and the intractability of abiding puzzles. Students gathered around a difficulty wear the look of wide-eyed children, while instructors often summon their own innocence, antic and animated: "Why *would* Plato banish the poets?" "Are there other reasons for Hamlet's delay?" It's not hard to see why the advanced seminar or the honors tutorial might seem a cave of indulgence. At the same time, it can appear a special zone reserved for initiates and experts. The issue is more than exclusive vocabulary. It's a matter of tone, gesture, the accents of skepticism, the eruptive laughter for no apparent reason. You needn't be an ethnographer to take up the outside view and to see these practices as local rituals: to join the seminar is to belong to a culture.

Those who don't belong to the culture remain conscious of its privilege. The everyday humanist often carries an image of professional authority as a sacred mystique. Joyce's Leopold Bloom, for instance, moves through the Dublin of *Ulysses* absorbed by the limits of the knowable. There is the vast universe and the immense vocabulary that comprehends it. There is, for instance, parallax:

> After one. Timeball on the ballast office is down. Dunsink time. Fascinating little book that is of sir Robert Ball's. Parallax. I never exactly understood. There's a priest. Could ask him. Par it's Greek: parallel, parallax.[1]

Some pages, but only a few moments, later, the musing resumes:

> Now that I come to think of it that ball falls at Greenwich time. It's the clock is worked by an electric wire from Dunsink. Must go out there some first Saturday of the month. If I could get an introduction to professor Joly or learn up something about his family. That would do to: man always feels complimented.

Flattery where least expected. Nobleman proud to be descended from some king's mistress. His foremother. Lay it on with a trowel. Cap in hand goes through the land. Not go in and blurt out what you know you're not to: what's parallax? Show this gentleman the door.[2]

As Bloom imagines blurting out his question to Professor Joly (Charles Jasper Joly, 1864–1906, Royal Astronomer of Ireland), he performs the self-chastening of an amateur who places legitimate knowledge far above, to be shared only among a class of special beings. And when he imagines his humiliation ("Show this man the door"), he accepts the boundary between his curiosity and sanctioned expertise. Yet his ruminations go unbroken. Among its other arcs and sparks, *Ulysses* is the epic of undampened curiosity.

The focus of Bloom's thought is worth marking. Parallax is a concept from science, drawn from astronomy, and through the long course of the day Bloom often returns to technical and scientific puzzles. Nothing is safe from his wondering. Indeed, the word "wonder" is insistent ("Wonder if she pronounces that right? Voglio"; "Wonder what kind is swanmeat?"; "Vats of porter wonderful"; of the cat, "Wonder if she could jump me"; and of a bat, "Wonder why they come out at night like mice"). He ponders history alongside biology, religion as well as opera, Shakespeare, the politics of Ireland, and the anatomy of classical statues. His home library, catalogued late in the novel, includes *Shakespeare's Works*, *Thoughts from Spinoza*, *Voyages in China*, *Short but Plain Elements of Geometry*, the *History of the Russo-Turkish War*.

Bloom is the everyday humanist, one exemplary case. The reach of his curiosity reveals a quiet insurgency: it is no respecter of boundaries. Questions of engineering and chemistry are as inviting as history, philosophy, and music. His case helps us to see that an everyday humanities not only disregards the borders of disciplines; it scarcely notices a difference between science and "softer" subjects. Because my own partisanship insists on seeing the "humanities-in-science" as well as the "science-in-humanities," I take Joyce's Bloom as friend and ally.

He is also an opening toward reconsideration of the contrast between engineering and bricolage, devised by Claude Lévi-Strauss.

In the chapter on "The Science of the Concrete" in *The Savage Mind*, Lévi-Strauss aims to recover techniques of knowledge as practiced in Neolithic societies, which he recognizes as "prior" rather than "primitive." The science of the concrete is not failed, immature, or undeveloped; it's merely a different style of knowing, one of the "two distinct modes of scientific thought."[3] The other is ours. To elucidate the difference Lévi-Strauss introduces the famous contrast.

Modern science, he proposes, applies a system of "engineering." It formulates a "project," deploying instruments, materials and procedures toward that end. If a tool or a substance is lacking, then it must be found. What governs the task of science is the *concept*, "the structures which it is constantly elaborating and which are its hypotheses and theories."[4] The scientist-as-engineer will adjust the concepts as they meet reality, but they are always the directing agent of success and failure, truth and falsity. For an "engineering" science, the idea is prior, the instrument a secondary necessity.

Bricolage works with what it happens to find, making do with pieces of the world that happen to appear. Accidents of experience, not the abstractions of science, guide the course of action. The bricoleur must always improvise: "His universe of instruments is closed and the rules of his game are always to make do with 'whatever is at hand,' that is to say with a set of tools and materials which is always finite."[5] Bricolage turns old objects to present uses; it draws on the "collection of oddments left over from human endeavours." So, for instance, a bricoleur finds a piece of wood and then responds to its contingencies: "A particular cube of oak could be a wedge to make up for the inadequate length of a plank of pine or it could be a pedestal—which would allow the grain and polish of the old wood to show to advantage."[6] The tasks may never be completed; they may lack coherence and elegance; but they respond to the immediacies of our encounter with the sensible world.

The success of Lévi-Strauss's distinction has always exceeded its clarity. He himself admits that the distinction is "less absolute"[7] than may first appear: science too faces the constraints of accident and the limits of materials. But where the insight can be newly generative is in what it suggests for the "discipline" of knowledge. Engineer vs. bricoleur captures a contrast in both the intentions and habits of inquiry. Bricolage is indifferent to protocols and procedures, to norms of evidence and the stamp of certification. Most fundamentally, the two orientations differ on the question of "project."

It had been Sartre (Jean-Paul), above all others, who had pressed the importance of the idea: *project* as the choice of ends, the adjustment of means to ends, the condition of freedom, and the foundation of action. A decisive step in Lévi-Strauss, and part of the contra-Sartrean polemic of *The Savage Mind*, is to posit bricolage, its accidental materials and tools, as bearing "no relation to the current project, or indeed to any particular project." The means of the bricoleur "cannot therefore be defined in terms of a project."[8] This contrast, a cardinal dispute of the early sixties, marks a nexus in twentieth-century thought. For our purposes here, the challenge of Lévi-Strauss to Sartre—the claims of "whatever is at hand" against the concept-guided project—offers a chance to rethink the "parallel modes of acquiring knowledge."[9]

Joyce's Bloom gives texture to the theory. He is knowledge-hungry but moves through life without a method of inquiry or even a subject matter. What quickens him is simply a disposition ("I wonder"). As with the bricolage of the savage mind, he draws on the "oddments" that fall in his path: an overheard word, a signboard, a scrap of newspaper. But unlike the Neolithic brico-leur, he knows very well that the universe of knowledge has been organized by experts and specialists with their projects. In the case of "parallax," Bloom is respectful of the authority of Professor Joly, but also cynical about an approach to the master ("learn up something about his family"; "Lay it on with a trowel"). As *Ulysses* unfolds, it goes further in its resistance to the sheen of credentials. In the National Library, Stephen Dedalus, unknown and unpublished, pokes the eyes of the guardians of Shakespeare, defying the caution of their views. In "Cyclops," the Rabelaisian narrator eviscerates the academic dignitary come to observe the execution of Robert Emmett, merely by naming him and his title; "Kriegfried Ueberallgemein," "Nationalgymnasiummuseumsanatoriumandsuspensoriumsordinary privatdocentgeneralhistoryspecialprofessordoctor."[10] The authorities are visible and humorless; Bloom and Dedalus pursue knowledge in the interstices.

What Joyce illuminates is the situation of an everyday humanities that is unrepentant, even as it understands the weight of academic authority. They live side by side, the disciplines and the un-disciplined inquirers. But it remains a stubborn question: what's at stake in the pursuit of knowledge without "discipline"—without credential, procedure, and precedent?

After Hours: Book Clubs and Living History

You can begin to answer by visiting any local book club, or for that matter, by finding a group online. They assemble, you find, in quite different ways. Part of the zip and lilt of the *Jane Austen Book Club* comes from the frank admission of many motives. You can be there because you've always loved the fiction, or because you meant to return to the books, or finally to finish them, or because you like the company or you're restless or lonely, or because you want to know more and be better. You may enter shyly, assured by remembering that you can always leave when you please. No one has signed you up or in for life.

The rooms—real or virtual—claim none of the aura of academic settings. Nor, crucially, do they depend on the voice of authority. The question of intellectual democracy always hovers in the air, whether or not it is explicitly voiced. Often it is. The group will decide which day of the week suits it best, which book to select for the next meeting, and who, if anyone, should introduce the discussion. Sometimes a recognized leader, perhaps the founding spirit behind the club, will emerge. But the dominating ethic is an openness, stretched as far as possible, letting all opinions into the mix until something breaks down, and the group awkwardly tries to mend itself.

The small-scale sociology of the book club is as interesting as it is subterranean. There are good reasons to keep self-consciousness at bay, and not to press questions of procedure and policy. Invariably, distinctions among the members emerge. These are people here. Someone is better informed, someone is funny, someone never finishes the book, someone brings up extraneous detail, someone—that one—talks too much. Because the members are usually adults, and usually somewhat more adult adults, they hope to avoid the social catastrophes of a teenage clique. Polite requests are made, cautious gestures. If warning becomes necessary, phone calls and emails will be exchanged, and someone, or some two, may carefully approach someone else.

In fact, the awkwardnesses seem rare. They tend not to diminish enthusiasm. The records show that club membership changes slowly; dropout rates are low; more than half of members participate for two to three years. Part of what sustains the groups is exactly their a-professionalism, the determination to avoid rigid standards of conversation or measured benchmarks of achievement, but also to mute any statement of goals. When asked, participants say such things as "I love to read," "It's a way to meet new people," "I want to get back to literature," "I've been meaning to catch up on new books." The last comment carries implications of its own. A strong bias runs toward contemporary fiction, not only living writers, but their latest productions. Although many reports mention a member who wants to "go back to the classics" and a good number of groups keep a proportion of "older literature," books are frequently chosen because they promise insight into the way we live now. Reviews in major papers are quoted and given possibly undue authority. The desire to stay current with the currents of culture has a binding force for most participants; it helps to minimize the unevenness of academic background and reading experience.

Seen through the norms of academic literary study, the discussions can seem careless of the object, the text itself. The monthly book often serves as a prod to associations, memories, preferences. Personal reactions are coin of this realm; the words "liked" and "didn't like" hang in the air. Why should they not? Absent any interest in defining a discipline or asserting a professionalism, the conversation can enjoy its license. The very disagreements—"Do you call that ending realistic?" or "How can you know it shows anxiety about sexuality?"—register the open terms that are inviting to members. Irritation is a fair price to pay for the freedom of thought and the rights of curiosity. In the clubs, it's common to hear from someone who began with disappointment in the book or even anger toward it, but who then says, "I enjoy it more after our discussion." Usually, the change of heart is not cast as "I understand it now," but rather as "I didn't realize there was so much in it."

What do the discussants want from their discussions? A too immediate answer is to say that the group searches for (some of) the meaning of the text, or at least its personal meaning to individuals. Listening more patiently to the participants, though, we find it's not typically an arrival at understanding that stirs the effort—not the achievement of some hard kernel of insight. What keeps conversation alive is less approach to a meaning than the opening of a flexible web of perspectives and contexts and tracks for continuing exchange ("What I still don't see is ...," "Can we talk about the incident by the seaside?", "What's the character of Martha doing in the book?"). Not convergence, but diffusion along many lines of suggestion, revision, comic banter. Because the academic humanities remain haunted by images of advance or progress—toward more precise concepts, more rigorous conclusions—we tend to repress our own habits, good habits, of dispersed conversation, of slowly focusing or unfocused chatter. Orderless talk and thought—throwing out an idea, teasing it, being thrown a different one, staying provisional, speculative, over-general, undercertain—these are not only the preconditions to rigorous thought; they underlie the vocation of thought itself. The informality of the book club captures a truth about the seminar room that we do well not to deny or reprove.

Before all, it's the question of value that marks the in-discipline of the book club. A central element of socialization into the academy involves learning a chaste use of praise and blame. It's fair to be a professorial partisan of Vermeer, Austen, and Wittgenstein, but only to a limited extent. Within the university, the claim of value is an ornament or a penumbra, not the justifying task. We teach, and show, that it should not intrude on the labor of interpretation and contextualization. In university settings, the naming of value—the greatness of Shakespeare, say—appears as much *quoted* as asserted. It can often appear risky or taboo. Even when delivered with passion and conviction, celebration (or denigration) comes with self-consciousness; everyone knows that expressions of value are laden with assumptions, that they are always vulnerable to theoretically sophisticated critique.

Value in the book club, on the other hand, is an engine of conversation and a reason to meet in the first place. It carries no special quiver of anxiety. "I liked Helen more than Margaret" is a sentence that even young university students know to mock. But within the everyday life of a book club, the contrast between personal preference and the objectivity of the text is untroubling. Furthermore, it doesn't disable conversation. Two members can express an irreconcilable difference of opinion ("hated it," "loved it"), without ruffling the mood any more than if they'd differed over sardines or squash. And what exactly is wrong with this? Without settling on precepts or theories, the conversation is still capable of thinking about itself. Someone will ask for more evidence in the words; another may speculate about the author's deeper motives. They may, or may not, press the divergence between these ways of thinking and talking.

Here it will be helpful to place the Book Club alongside the equally flourishing practice of Living History. In the one, participants gather in comfortable interiors that encourage the intimacy of face-to-face exchange, inevitably with limits on the size of the group. Living History, on the other hand, depends almost always on visibility in the public realm. This is not only because the re-enactment of events is typically on the large scale—battles, dances, flotillas—but also because the stagings are designed to attract an audience, including school groups. With resources drawn from the Internet, ambitions have grown quickly. Now you regularly find complex logistical arrangements—for the making of costumes, the distribution of armaments, the schedule of events, the availability of video—that show a high degree of organizational planning.

The movement attracts its share of condescension and caricature. The sight of families in full Viking garb, carrying weaponry at dangerous angles, is ripe for lampooning. Yet it's clear that the re-enactors possess a conviction that remains undeterred by either embarrassment or cynical dismissal. The 10th Essex Regiment Living History Group speaks in representative tones:

> Our motto is "Education, not Entertainment"—and we are keen to express the fact that "whilst we don't do it for fun, we have fun whilst we do it." Chalke Valley History Festival has to be one of our best events so far—not only for the fact that we had so many appreciative and interested parties pass through our encampment but also because the entire experience, from the trench build through the interpretation to the take-down and pack-up was something we won't forget—and we very much hope that we can do it all again next year![11]

What distinguishes the Living History movement is the emphatic centrality of "experience," of sensory presence to a simulacrum of the past. This is another area where academic reaction becomes queasy.

The rigors of scholarly training depend, rightly so, on the sublimation of immediate desires, on an intellectual austerity that depends on the deferral of other satisfactions. Undergraduate talk of epiphany or revelation, of passion or excitement, is benignly tolerated as the early mist of enthusiasm that will dissipate under the longer light of graduate study. The contrast between professional and amateur regularly turns on contrasting views of the rights of emotion.

This book means to put professionalism in context and in question, and the claim of experience is a prominent issue. Those who practice the everyday humanities are often not only unapologetic but even outspoken about the need for a full-bodied immersion in their subjects, their passions. Living historians, sometimes explicitly, and sometimes not, affirm the unity of knowledge and experience; the depth of their insistence might encourage reconsideration of professional self-fashioning. The picture of the professor as elite, effete, desiccated, and un-matey, is unfair and unfounded. We eat; we weep. And yet, though exceptions are many, the norms of professional instruction find the "experiential" occasions—student performances, recitations, etc.—frivolous, tedious, and never more than secondary accompaniments. Art historians will demand an encounter with the objects themselves, as historians of music depend on acts of close listening. But even these attentive acts are preliminary to the tasks of research, teaching, and writing: you see, you listen, in order to build an argument, construct a narrative, or complete a bibliography. There may be more to learn from the thriving world of Living History, namely that a prolonged experience that is visual, audial, and gestural, not simply linguistic/conceptual, may be a means to a pedagogical end, and also an end in itself, an enlargement and refinement of a thinking–feeling complex. The everyday humanities sustain a still living ideal of pleasure-in-instruction, whose harmless sound shouldn't disguise its challenge to the dominant professionalism.

A further aspect of Living History will carry us to a next concern. This is its characteristic division into areas of emphasis and specialization. Partly, these follow familiar styles of periodization; but partly, they reflect the spontaneity of an emerging subculture. Military re-enactments stand in clear majority, but other groups concentrating on other practices are plentiful and easy to locate, among them (in the UK): the Regency Assembly, the Victorian Photographer, Feudals (Normans),

Norwich Historical Dance. What the groups share, military and pacific, is a dedicated focus on historical details: dress, implements, setting. A program of research belongs to almost all of them, and over time the density of detail increases markedly. Some members concentrate on one area, some on another; a spirit of collaboration is consistently evident.

In one respect, the groups exist as mirror images of academic practice. They establish areas of inquiry and boundaries of research; they preserve their displays, often deposited on the Internet, and maintain records of achievement. They also allow for the narrowing interests of individuals, as specialized as any university professor. One difference, of course, is that while academic departments struggle against contraction and must husband tight budgets, many Living History groups grow apace and prosper. Both those who perform for hire and those who rely on their own funding and enthusiasm ride the support of popularity; they exist just to the extent that participants and audiences care to commit some weekends. Then, too, the groups can draw strength from flexible goals and relaxed criteria of success.

At the same time, a consciousness of expert authority elsewhere is an abiding feature of the groups. They typically seem more at ease presenting themselves as hobbyists, seriously and playfully dedicated to the task, but reluctant to overstate credentials or claims. It's not uncommon for doctorate-holding professionals to be consulted, though even with that sanction, the groups avoid pretension to academic achievement. But alongside the open self-chastening ("We shouldn't claim to be experts") is found the assertion of the rights of curiosity and the interest of their subject. Most groups hold to the significance of their contribution and can parry professorial demands by insisting on the pleasures of "authenticity," however far it reaches. Comitatus, to take one case, offers itself as "Britain's leading Late Roman re-enactment group helping to set a new standard in historical authenticity" and notes that its members "are dedicated enthusiasts who enjoy what they do and have a reputation for passing on this passion to the public! Members of the public frequently join us as members after seeing the displays, and we are always open to new recruits."[12] These claims and tones are common. They also chime with claims in what must be our own most-provoking example.

Wiki-Truth

Wikipedia is both a test case for the everyday humanities and a singular instance. It promotes itself, and knows itself, as the free encyclopedia, produced by anyone, open to all, and under that banner, its rise has been legendary. Granted, the achievement is not unprecedented. Other epochs have admired equally legendary achievements: the *Encyclopédie* of Diderot and Rameau, compiled and published in the later eighteenth century, and the *Oxford English Dictionary* (OED) begun in 1857 and ongoing. *Wikipedia* belongs to that tradition, but also exceeds it. Not merely the differences in scale—by its own proud breathless account, more than hundred times the words of *Encyclopedia Britannica*—but also the rapidity of its growth. It became a presence on the Internet in just a few years; it became globally inescapable within just a few more.

A more immediate precedent is the movement of Free and Open-Source Software (FOSS), which developed in the eighties and nineties. Software that could be used for any purposes, that could be edited for continuous improvement, that could be used and circulated freely, in the original or changed version—these were the generating events. They were at once technical and social/ethical. Jimmy Wales, one of the two founders of *Wikipedia*, recalled his moment of recognition:

> one of the things that I noticed is that in the humanities, a lot of people were collaborating in *discussions*, while in programming, something different was going on. People weren't just talking about programming, they were working to build things of value.[13]

The irony is illuminating. Wales was celebrating the can-do, let's-get-on-with-it attitude of programmers. And yet the history of *Wikipedia* has enacted a movement toward the other pole of his contrast. The technical breakthrough—the invention of the "wiki" tool that allows real-time collaborative editing—has been elaborated and refined. But its character hasn't fundamentally changed since the turn of the millennium. On the other hand, the first decade and a half of *Wikipedia* has brought advances and provocations that should be seen within the frame of the humanities as Wales portrays them here: a "lot of people" "collaborating in discussions." The social force of *Wikipedia* and its intellectual challenge lie in the fearsome complexity of that collaboration.

In motto and practice as "the free encyclopedia that anyone can edit,"[14] *Wikipedia* extends the principles of open-source software. Because it is an encyclopedia, its substance is, in principle, the full reach of knowledge. But because "anyone can edit" the text, what constitutes knowledge—as a concept and a whole, and as finite particular pieces of the known—is perpetually up for grabs. No one who changes the encyclopedia is required to confirm a credential or a degree, or to give a name or an age. The attack on the authority of sanctioned expertise is at once vast and self-conscious.

The origins are legendary for good reason. After early success in the Internet economy, Jimmy Wales ("Jimbo") approached Larry Sanger (doctoral student in philosophy) with the idea of an online encyclopedia. In its first version, known as *Nupedia*, an array of scholars was asked to produce essays that would be definitive and readily available. Led by an advisory board composed of "mostly Ph.D. professors but also a good many other highly-experienced professionals," it would be an "academically-respectable project" depending on "experts in their fields."[15] *Reliability* was the watchword. Within an ocean of Internetic babble and blog, *Nupedia* meant to validate its credibility, both through its recognized authorities and a rigorous seven-step review: "Uncredentialed people *could* (and did) participate in Nupedia, particularly as writers and copyeditors, but it was pretty painful for most of them to get articles through the elaborate system" (Sanger,"Early History of Wikipedia"). The nub is exactly here. Sanger's principle, well established by the pre-Internet traditions of the academy, inevitably met practical difficulties. Was there reason to doubt it would? Within the sliced and slivered life of the university, expertise cannot be furnished on request; nor can it always be delivered on time. The demand for rigor requires patience, and the lure of novelty isn't strong enough to change the duration of research. Plausible in principle, the idea stumbled in practice. The scholars (surprise!) missed deadlines. Under the weight of the seven steps of review, entries accumulated much too slowly. Apart from its handy delivery on computer screens, *Nupedia* could not expect to grow faster than *Britannica*. While the two editors were waiting, they devised the parallel project, the parent-devouring child.

The audacious step was to suspend the two root principles (expertise and review) and open the gate-flooding alternative (editing by "anyone"), whose success, we have every reason to believe, startled them. *Wikipedia* launched in January, 2001. It had accumulated roughly 600 articles by the end of the month, 3,900 in May, 11,000 by October. When I first drafted this chapter in February 2015, it had 4,726,997 articles in English, and when we arrived at copy-editing in April 2017, it had 5,348,439—actually, I mean 5,368,155. Few have been unimpressed by the growth, but many have worried about reliability. Sanger himself remained a leading skeptic even after the project became inescapably visible and addictively used. Whether or not the encyclopedia *was* unreliable, he argues, it was *seen as* unreliable. For him, the central difficulty is clear:

> as a community, Wikipedia lacks the habit or tradition of respect for expertise. As a community, far from being elitist (which would, in this context, mean *excluding* the unwashed masses), it is *anti*-elitist (which, in this context, means that expertise is not accorded any special respect, and snubs and disrespect of expertise is tolerated).[16]

Those with credentials, suggests Sanger, will keep away from *Wikipedia*, not wanting to invite critique from "nonexperts." Years into the phase of "anyone can edit," Sanger was calling for an advisory board that would oversee a privileged section of the encyclopedia, ring-fencing it with the reassurance of credibility.

It's not that Sanger's objections have disappeared. But at some point early in the second decade of the new millennium, consulting *Wikipedia* became second nature at every level of the academy. Most who live in universities can recall how recently they considered it academically radioactive, how important it seemed to warn students away from the site. Speaking for myself, I can't quite fix the moment when I put aside the gymnastics of self-justification and just clicked. But it does seem right to face the issue and to admit the comeuppance that the corps of scholars has endured. What's at stake hasn't been a yielding to the student-driven wave of acceptance. Nor has it been simply the lowering of a bar. What seems quietly to have changed is the terms of reliability itself. We may have learned more about what we want to know and how we are prepared to know it.

Wikipedia is vulnerable to initial error, as well as to the malice of vandalism. But the shock has been the discovery in practice of what was predicted in theory, namely that many eyes, very many eyes, are likely to correct errors quickly. Part of the quick-forming legend gathers around the study conducted by *Nature* in 2005. The conclusion was that *Wikipedia* and *Britannica* achieved roughly comparable levels of reliability: for articles on topics in science, there were on average four errors in a *Wikipedia* entry and about three in *Britannica*.[17] Flurries ensued. *Britannica* challenged the findings, while *Wikipedia* took pride in quickly correcting any mistakes the study had uncovered. Since that time, other studies have reached various conclusions. In some fields of science, the encyclopedia has won endorsement for technical accuracy, in others not. The telling issue is that, on the whole, articles have improved over time. Consciousness of risks of error and the dedication of core contributors make it likely that the arc of improvement will rise, and indeed, rise far more quickly because of the never-sleeping and ongoing system of revision.

Improvement on the whole, but inadequacy, even embarrassment, in many parts. The editing has no terminus; articles that have won admiration can lose it overnight; new articles can appear through the singular passions of anonymous individuals. From the moment one enters the editing template, there are few constraints on what can be said or unsaid. One result is that the radical unevenness—in reliability, in style, in usefulness—is not a sign of an immaturity that will disappear. Unevenness is the condition of the project. Anyone who navigates regularly and randomly through the pages has the experience of finding a series of helpful items speedily negotiated, only to arrive at a dead end where information drains to a minimum, or commits error, or disappears.

Wikipedia challenges the procedures of knowledge, its aims toward steady convergence, its traditional justifications. The problem is not that knowledge is in motion. It always has been. Academic research takes its deepest pride in remaining alive to change. In *Wikipedia*, however, the motion of knowledge is unpredictable, erratic, sometimes unintelligible, or willfully unaccommodating.

Norms of what constitutes trusted knowledge have been suspended—and also what constitutes reasonable dispute. Think only of the expected concerns in an academic evaluation, for instance at the time of appointment or annual review: the worry that the candidate has only published in second-rank journals, or has not established her own voice apart from her collaborators, or is depending too heavily on the precedents of a mentor. The adjectives of appraisal may be imprecise. The work is "fresh" or "derivative," "speculative" or "definitive," "under-theorized" or "period-bound." These are words like others. If we accept and employ them in deliberations, it's not because their definitions are crisp, but because we have learned how to exchange them as tools of appraisal. When they are challenged, we resort to other words, no less vulnerable, but belonging to established practices also accepted, much as we have accepted norms of annotation and acknowledgement. Academic life, as we well know, is an exercise in socialization, not only to protocols of research and teaching, but also to the vocabulary of evaluation.

Such habits of normalization are resisted on *Wikipedia*. On March 13, 2015, you would have found that "The *Wikipedia* community has developed many policies and guidelines to improve the encyclopedia; however, it is not a formal requirement to be familiar with them before contributing. (http://en.wikipedia.org/wiki/Wikipedia:About)." In more colorful tones on that same day, you would have read that "On Wikipedia, **there are no cops**. Everyone is an editor. While editors may possess different abilities before they edit Wikipedia, and editors may be granted different abilities after they edit Wikipedia, that does not mean they are better than other editors." The result is that gate-keeping is thrust to a low priority, not much more than an embarrassing necessity. The invitation to "anyone" to join the editorial project and to make changes that appear immediately means that (almost) all appraisal is after the fact. It's an arrangement that prepares for legendary mis-adventure. The announcement of the deaths of Ted Kennedy and Miley Cyrus, the claims that Tony Blair hung posters of Hitler, the insinuations about the golfer Fuzzy Zoller, the identification of John Seigenthaler as suspect in the Kennedy assassination: these are cele-brated cases. The encyclopedia has taken steps—including the use of automated algorithms—to prevent obvious vandalism. Still, no one denies that inadvertent errors and malicious distortions can till a fertile field.

The vulnerability is an effect of anchored commitments to the social practice of openness: open to the non-credentialed, the insomniac, the obsessive, the visionary, the eccentric. As far as possible, the goal has been to accept the dangers of flexibility:

Wikipedia has no firm rules: Wikipedia has policies and guidelines, but they are not carved in stone; their content and interpretation can evolve over time. Their principles and spirit matter more than their literal wording, and sometimes improving Wikipedia requires making an exception. Be bold but not reckless in updating articles, and do not agonize about making mistakes.[18] (March 13, 2015)

What comes quickly into question is the knowledge-giving community itself. The principle, drawn from open-source software, is that a multitude can be a self-regulating apparatus; it can offer powers of information-gathering and dissemination on a scale beyond previous efforts, within or without the university. But the multitude cannot silence the worries over legitimacy. Not only are there many errors of ignorance or incompetence; the threat of opportunism is ever near. Individuals or organizations can insert words of praise into an entry under their own names; political offices have been found erasing mention of their questionable practices; passionate social campaigners will disregard principles of neutrality; enthusiasts will brighten the tone in descriptions of cherished works of art. *Wikipedia* attracts and to a notable extent allows trolls. Then, apart from malice, there are entries no one would accept as useful: these can be earnest accounts of arcane personal enthusiasms, or they can simply be too brief or too badly worded to illuminate anything about something. Many pages on the site describe best practices of writing, responding, and editing. But who could have doubted that anonymous collective composition would yield not only variable quality of content but also great variability in tone and the rhetoric of exposition?

It's worth probing the worry over reliability. What, after all, are we worried about, we humanists in particular? Surely, the concern is not about incorrect interpretation, which the site explicitly discourages, though it can never be fully avoided. Critics and scholars are well accustomed to endless refinements of interpretation; and weak suggestions in an entry differ only in degree from weaknesses met and corrected in the classroom. More to the point is a wariness before the fact world in *Wikipedia*: dates, titles, places. That these could be wrong within an encyclopedia, even temporarily, seems a violation of sacred secular principle. If errors like these can be made, how can anything else be trusted? This (real) worry tells us something about the place of "fact" within the humanities. Because many think of interpretation as our central justifying activity, we tend to neglect (or more likely simplify) the place of fact. We can take too much for granted that art historians need to know the provenance of painting, that biblical scholars must indicate the source on which their argument rests, that literary scholars and musicologists depend on the integrity of their texts. We incline to see scientists as the committed empiricists, but the humanities too depend on observation, record, and report. Think only of the crucial place of the example, the quotation, the precisely identified fragment of a work (canvas, score, text). These may seem the unglamorous bits within ambitious interpretations. But they remind us of the science-in-humanities, the place of empirics. The noisy controversies over reliability in *Wikipedia* have usefully opened this aspect of the humanities to clearer view.

The controversies over reliability are media-enticing. Mistakes are exciting; so too is the relative success in rapid self-correction that such large-scale communities can provide. But a more significant event has been overlooked: the change in the very domain of knowledge, of what counts as, and constitutes, knowledge. Jimmy Wales asked his audience to "Imagine a world in which every single human being can freely share in the sum of all knowledge."[19] The world, wrote Wittgenstein, "is the totality of facts."[20] Wales here suggests a similar world picture: a universe of knowable facts that can be recorded, edited, and amplified by a community large enough and engaged enough to survey the total field.

But, in fact, the short history of *Wikipedia* has shown not only that knowledge has no "sum," but that its units, the items of knowledge, have no standard form. Was it a surprise to the founders—most likely yes—that their encyclopedia would depart so fully from conventions of content, from any consistent framework that would arrange familiar items to query: persons, minerals, and animals; places and important proper names; events and texts and scientific terms, etc.? From its earliest days, *Wikipedia* indeed included these canonical topics, as of course it must. So under the heading "Why Wikipedia is not a Dictionary,"[21] you find this characterization of a fit subject for an entry, namely, "a person, or a people, a concept, a place, an event, a thing etc. that their title can *denote*. The article octopus is about the animal: its physiology, its use as food, its scientific classification, and so forth." So far, so standard. The surprise lies in the changes it works on the canons of knowledge.

~~The first change was simply to enlarge the canon to a scale that had~~ been unimaginable, to accept entries that would have seemed too meager or wasteful or *enthusiastic*. I say "simply," but the effect is complex. That the Internet removed limits on the number of topics, that the seventeen or twenty-seven or thirty-six volumes of the *World Book Encyclopedia* came to seem paltry, that the range of Wales's contributors, unpaid and unconstrained, grew and grew again—these no longer new circumstances allowed the rhetoric to shift from "significant knowledge" to "all knowledge"—what Wales calls "the sum." For instance, of the many battles in the American Civil War, a choice was traditionally made as to which deserved a separate entry. But *Wikipedia* can open toward a comprehensive list, including, say, the battles of Dry Wood Creek, and the battle of Blackburn's Ford—neither of which has earned an entry in the online *Britannica*. Similarly, minor agents in history can receive the dignity of heading. So Jenny Geddes enters *Wikipedia*, named as the Scottish market trader said to have precipitated the Wars of the Three Kingdoms by casting her stool at a clergyman. The shift is still more notable in the opening to mass and popular culture. An early controversy concerned how many episodes of *Buffy the Vampire Slayer* should be included. The concern naturally was that committed viewers would generate great bodies of text, with endless detail out of all proportion to entries on sober subjects such as the Periodic Table or the Hanseatic League.

Wikipedia and the Invention of Knowledge

It brings us to the second change, less visible or predictable but more consequential. Here, the decision to accept all and every *Buffy* is indicative. On August 12, 2016, an entry on the episode "Seeing Red" began as follows:

> "**Seeing Red**" is the 19th episode of season 6 of the television series <u>Buffy the Vampire Slayer</u>. In North America, this episode was somehow <u>syndicated</u> onto <u>UPN</u> affiliates a week early by accident. Although none of them broadcast the episode by mistake,

the episode was leaked onto the internet more than a week before it was slated to air. The episode was also noted for its drastic and controversial content, being the only episode of the series to air at an alternate time on the Canadian family network YTV.[22]

Not everyone needs to know this, but they are many more than will read this book of mine. Because anyone can edit a page, there is no limit to the micro-scale of information. Each iota is fair subject for editorial amplification. Further, it requires no attention from the uninitiated or uninterested, who will click on different links, each opening optional vistas that have no weight on the bookshelf, no added expense for the library. It's more than a question of confusing hierarchies of "high" and "low," the time-sanctioned and the very latest. It's a deeper question about what can count as an object of inquiry.

Let's take, for instance, the "tie-in," that small rat-a-tat-tat of commercial culture. Any search for the term quickly finds dictionaries that offer terse definition. The online *Cambridge Dictionary* delineates "a product such as a toy or book that is related to a film, television programme, etc." Other dictionaries offer variations on this defintion, but in their midst on the Google search (as the second site to display in mid-August 2016) appears *Wikipedia*. Its entry begins with a definition close to others, but it then continues: "Tie-ins are authorized by the owners of the original property, and are a form of cross-promotion used primarily to generate additional income from that property and to promote its visibility." This one step marks the passage from dictionary to encyclopedia, from an elucidation of the word (the verbal meaning of "tie-in") to information on its use, context, and purpose. The entry goes on for several hundred words, describing the "Types" (informing us, for instance, that "one to two percent of an audience of a film will buy its novelization") and its "Revenue and Structure," ending with links to "Cross media marketing," "Media franchise," "Merchandising," "Expanded Universe," and "Toyetic."

Once an unlikely candidate for recognition (and nowhere to be found in *Britannica*), the "tie-in" receives the dignity of inquiry. It too belongs to the universe of the knowable. The force of the example is only partly its challenge to the distinction between significant and insignificant subjects. At least as important is how such cases unsettle the contrast between dictionary and encyclopedia. *Wikipedia* entries typically begin in the mode of definition, which then opens in a second or third sentence to widening content (often emphasizing histories and varieties). Because of its two crucial magnitudes—the immensity of space and the vast community of editors—words that might have been fated to live only in dictionaries enter the network of encyclopedic knowledge.

"Anyone Can Edit": The Social Life of Polylogue

Of the two magnitudes, it's the second that makes the major difference. The demographic spread of the editors is notoriously skewed: toward English-language speakers, toward men, toward the technologically engaged. And then within the large population of those who contribute and revise, a relatively small group remains active. Although "Anyone Can Edit," not everyone does. But while this accepted in-discipline opens the risks of reliability, bias, and the possibilities for error, inadvertent or intentional, it also brings interest and inquiry near to one another. Individuals or groups take up a knowledge project that can be pursued over years. The result is the notorious discrepancy in length, tone, and satisfaction of individual entries.

But the second result of wide participation is the invention of new objects of knowledge. Aspects of the world that had not qualified for encyclopedic recognition now exist on equal clickable footing. A distinctive pattern is the continual subdivision of a unit of inquiry. The passage from "Buffy the Vampire Slayer" to the "List of Buffy the Vampire Slayer Episodes" to "Season 6 2001–2002" to "Seeing Red" gives the standard movement toward ever more focused particulars. Under the heading of "Writing" within "Seeing Red," you find an account of a panel discussion that addressed the difficulty of spraying Tara's blood onto Willow's shirt. Taking a different route, during any given lunch hour, the entry on Samuel Johnson brings us, unsurprisingly, to a mention of his travel narrative, *A Journey to the Western Islands of Scotland*. The journey receives a full entry in its own right, including mention of Monboddo House, where Johnson and Boswell paid a visit to Lord Monboddo. Already, we are beyond the reach of other encyclopedias, and by the time we click through Monboddo House to "garderobe" (medieval storeroom, wardrobe, latrine), we find *Wikipedia* in full micro glory.

The circuit moves just as strongly in the other direction: toward new classes, groups, and categories. The city of Geneva, for instance, is not only the occasion for independent recognition; it's also a node in an overlapping and reticulating network. Unchallengingly, the links open to entries on language and nationality ("Romany," the French-speaking region of the country), geography (the "Rhone," "Lake Geneva"), geo-economy ("Financial Centre"), political history ("Geneva Conventions," "List of mayors of Geneva"), and so on. But the city also falls within higher-level categories, equally accessible: ("Quality of Life," "Global Financial Centres Index," "List of most expensive cities for expatriate employers," and through another passageway, "List of Permanent Representatives of New Zealand to the United Nations in Geneva"). The creation of list-gathering entries, which has become a more visible feature of *Wikipedia*, adds a layer of complexity to the theory of knowledge that is only partly explicit in the stated aims of the project.

Another remark from Lévi-Strauss's *The Savage Mind* is to our purpose: "The proliferation of concepts, as in the case of technical languages, goes with more constant attention to properties of the world, with an interest that is more alert to possible distinctions which can be introduced between them."[23] "Proliferating concepts" may be the most significant change offered by *Wikipedia*, and they are far most disruptive than questions of reliability. That no a priori limits constrain the entries, that they can be as multiple (and as surprising) as the interests of "anyone," that new distinctions can be continually introduced—these are challenges to our understanding, not only of encyclopedias, but of knowledge itself. Very early in its history, *Wikipedia* has shown how inquiry can be radicalized in the two directions we have been following. It opens toward ever more particular probing and also toward new and shifting categories for containing particularity. Knowledge can be more precise and its clas-sifications more mobile. *Wikipedia* thus becomes a home both for the enthusiast pursuing specific texts, events, niceties, minutiae, and also for the ardent quester after new lists, categories, and classifications. Is this a transformation in the nature of inquiry or only an interesting evolution? The difference hardly matters, as long as we admit the radical extension in what can count as an object of knowledge and a path of serious inquiry.

Wikipedia, I say again, belongs to a long tradition within the humanities, its headlong assemblage of entries looking back at least as far the gathering of classical texts during the fourteenth- and fifteenth-century Italian Renaissance. The deep difference, of course, is social—the opening of editorship, in principle if not in perfect practice, to anyone with an Internet connection. The limited demographic reach of the editors should be stressed and overcome as far as possible. The tilt toward white, North-Atlantic, English-speaking males ensures an imbalance. But even within the skewed population, the challenges show themselves. The everyday humanities are at their most public and provocative in this collaborative, ever-changing, anyone-can-edit construction of knowledge.

Although the most famous of *Wikipedia*'s Five Pillars is its second (that the encyclopedia is "free content that anyone can use, edit, and distribute"), its first pillar had already tried to neutralize some likely threats: *Wikipedia* is neither an "experiment in anarchy or democracy" nor a "soapbox," "advertising platform," or "vanity press." The insistence is necessary because the social stakes are high. Given the commitment to universal access and input, the project will remain vulnerable. Yet, even as it makes a formal call for "respect and civility" (pillar three), the last of its grounding principles (pillar five) returns to the wiki inspiration: the absence of "firm rules" guiding the open collective. It can startle no one that its fifteen years have seen continuous wrangles, controversies, minor dust-ups, and major disagreements.

The few enunciated principles are self-consciously general and casual in tone, and they are at their most theoretically exposed in pillar number two:

> *Wikipedia* is written from a neutral point of view. We strive for articles that document and explain major points of views, giving due weight with respect to their prominence in an impartial tone. We avoid advocacy and we characterize information and issues rather than debate them. In some areas there may be just one well-recognized point of view; in others, we describe multiple points of view, presenting each accurately and in context

rather than as "the truth" or "the best view." All articles must
strive for verifiable accuracy, citing reliable, authoritative sources,
especially when the topic is controversial or is on living persons.
Editors' personal experiences, interpretations, or opinions do
not belong.[24]

The stiffness of tone fits the difficulty of the issue, a difficulty that the
entry on NPOV (Neutral Point of View) attempts to clarify: Neutrality
is not Objectivity. No effort should be made to escape the clash of
perspectives and rise to the detachment of a "view from nowhere."[25]
Rather the aim is to represent as "fairly, proportionately, and, as far as
possible, without editorial bias, all of the significant views that have
been published by reliable sources on a topic." Put only slightly differently, the goal is "to describe disputes, but not engage in them," and
always to aim towards a "tone" of neutrality, providing an "unbiased,
accurate, and proportionate representation of all positions included
in the article."[26]

The philosophic fragility of these positions is open and undisguised;
it requires scant recollection of twentieth-century debates in epistem-
ology, ethics, and aesthetics to find arguments against each of the
abstractions summoned to support the "pillar." The appeal to unbiased
accuracy, to fairness and proportion, only substitutes new questionable
foundations for the shaky structure of neutrality. Any brief encounter
with the "talk" pages linked to controversial articles (abortion, self-
harm, Julian Assange) will find waves of disagreement, and not only
about the tense subject itself, but also about the principles of neutrality
that are meant to stabilize the conversation. "Talk" goes foundational,
without finding secure justifications for one version of neutrality or
another. Debate, sometimes bitter, frequently gathers around the stated
goals of unbiased accuracy and "proportionate representation" which
are scarcely avoidable within the scope of 4,000 to 6,000 words. Anyone
who uses a mobile phone knows that information would be clearer,
richer, more *reliable*, on the landline. But the loss of information on
the cell—common enough to bring memorable errors, private and
public—is, we decide, almost always worth bearing. The portability
and ease are compensations for the epistemological static of a weak
connection. On a more consequential scale, this is our relationship
with *Wikipedia*. Its neutrality is an unrealizable ideal; the question of

its reliability can never be put to rest. Yet it has become as close to indispensable as any tool of inquiry we have.

In the fall of 2016, three researchers, Greenstein, Gu, and Zhu, published a working paper in the *Harvard Business Review*. It gave results of their study of the "bias" and "slant" in the politically inflected contributions of *Wikipedia* editors. Cataloguing thousands of instances over time, the study found that, as editors meet on contested terrain, they moved out of "segregated" communities of ideologically like-minded partisans and toward less extreme positions. The process was slow but detectable. Contributors tend to engage with opposing perspectives ("which we call the OA [Opposites Attract] effect"). The findings "also show that contributors moderate their contribution over time. The change in contributions is especially large for contributors who interact with articles that are more extreme." Put succinctly, "contributors with different political viewpoints tend to have dialogues with each other during their editing of contestable knowledge."[27]

These rosy conclusions may or may not be confirmed, but they do help clarify what's at stake in Wikipedian editorship. The achievement is not steady convergence and an approach toward the sum of knowledge. It's rather a noisy polylogue that never quietens down. The digest of edits preserved for each entry records not only the ideological exchange that Greenstein, Gu, and Zhu have found, but also a history of unruly deliberation. Species-borne, the irritations and stubbornness are likely to persist as long as people make and want *Wikipedia*. Any long look at the editing pages will find a preponderance of fair-minded inquiry, but will also find impasse that requires long exchange to resolve. And then, even after negotiation seems to have satisfied editors, a wound of resentment may reopen. The most difficult and revealing episodes occur when impasse can't be resolved through organic ongoing dialogue. The topic may then be removed from open editing, becoming "protected" or "semi-protected," as follows:

> in some particular circumstances, because of a specifically identified likelihood of damage resulting if editing is left open, some individual pages may need to be subject to technical restrictions (often only temporary but sometimes indefinitely)

on who is permitted to modify them. The placing of such restrictions on pages is called **protection**.

Protection can only be applied to or removed from pages by Wikipedia's *administrators,* although any user may *request* protection. Protection can be indefinite or expire after a specified time period.[28]

The imperfect society of editorship is a hallmark of *Wikipedia*. If the intervention of administrators seems a blight on the principle that "anyone can edit," this will not only be because one has over-idealized the project but also because one misses some of the exemplary lessons. That different contributors have different attainments and offer varying levels of insight was inevitable. But, of course, *Wikipedia* hardly stands alone as a vessel for discrepant ability in the generation of knowledge. The university, like all the schools that precede it, is streaked by differ- ence. Variability can be masked by the simplicity of credentials that suggest students have reached a level of competence or that professors cluster around a standard of excellence. Some of this naiveté is felt in Larry Sanger's clamor for contributors who hold the Ph.D. Fair enough to say that the range is far greater in *Wikipedia*, and that it allows for egregious failure that is less likely to appear inside the university. But the deeper point is that knowledge is always adjusting to limitation. Nostalgia for the authority in encyclopedias of the last generation ignores how quickly even distinguished judgments must be amended. It also ignores the function of an encyclopedia, its most important function, as initiation in a topic and spur to more inquiry, as a beginning to research. As a container of facts, *Wikipedia* will mislead very few researchers, though when it does so, the annoyance will be great. But as a widening and reticulating of the network of knowledge, its contribution is only starting to be felt. The democracy of inquiry will need perpetual adjustment, constant polylogue. But in just a few years it's become clear that the multitude has brought knowledge into narrow spaces where it had no interest in burrowing before and that an opening field has new categories of synthesis that only the churlish refuse to admire (while secretly using).

In the Magna Carta anniversary year 2015, Cornelia Parker displayed an art object on the mezzanine level of the British Library. It was an embroidery, extending almost 13 meters, of *Wikipedia*'s article on the

Magna Carta as it had appeared one year before the eight-hundredth anniversary, that is, on June 15, 2014. Parker recruited two hundred contributors, most of them prisoners, to embroider the eighty-seven sections into which the page was divided, including the blue links which point to related pages. Alongside the prisoners stitched many others, including activists, campaigners, artists, academics, and professional needleworkers. (The *Wikipedia* article about the embroidery of the *Wikipedia* entry notes that the piece contains a mark of blood from the editor of *The Guardian*, Alan Rusbridger, who pricked his stitching finger, and a tea stain left by a prisoner contributing to the work).

Parker described her aim as "to raise questions about where we are now with the principles laid down in the Magna Carta, and about the challenges to all kinds of freedoms that we face in the digital age. Like a Wikipedia article, this embroidery is multi-authored and full of many different voices."[29] These are lofty words, well earned, but they don't catch another element of the embroidery, namely, its binding comic force. As I took my tea break from research on these pages, I drifted almost daily down from the humanities reading room and past the installation. Nearly always I came across scenes of pointing and smiling, especially at the incongruities produced by the scale and by the contrast between the richly embroidered blue thread and the links on the right side of an entry's page. Often visitors opened the page on their phones, one act of collaboration set alongside another.

A clue might be taken from this recent work, lying in Parker's willingness to mix such wide differences of skill in the making of embroidery. Rank amateurs had their work displayed alongside the virtuosity from members of the Embroiders' Guild—a conspicuous, much-commented-on disparity. It's of course what *Wikipedia* itself permits, the inconsistencies of training, skill, or commitment. And inconsistency is always, after all, the condition of knowledge, the side-by-sidedness of trained refinement and the first fumbling attempts, with all varieties in between. The fear is that the most important thoughts will be crowded out. It's the fear in any seminar, and it can happen. Insight can be trounced by stubbornness, poor manners, or ignorance. But the greater risk is the self-enclosure of the initiated and the credentialed, which not only brings the heavy social cost of elite withdrawal; it also weakens the thought of those withdrawing. Parker's embroidery gives an image of a risk worth taking, indeed the risk *Wikipedia* has taken many times since I began typing this sentence.

Notes

1. James Joyce, *Ulysses* (New York: Random House, 1961), 154.
2. Ibid., 167.
3. Claude Lévi-Strauss, *The Savage Mind* (Chicago: University of Chicago Press, 1966), 15.
4. Ibid., 22.
5. Ibid., 17.
6. Ibid., 18–19.
7. Ibid., 19.
8. Ibid., 11.
9. Ibid., 13.
10. Joyce, *Ulysses*, 307.
11. http://www.10thessex.org/latest-news/archives/09-2013, accessed Sept. 30, 2013.
12. http://comitatus.net/, accessed May 17, 2017.
13. Quoted in Joseph Michael Reagle, Jr., *Good Faith Collaboration: The Culture of Wikipedia* (Cambridge, MA: MIT Press, 2010), 4.
14. https://en.wikipedia.org/wiki/Main_Page, accessed May 17, 2017.
15. https://features.slashdot.org/story/05/04/18/164213/the-early-history-of-nupedia-and-wikipedia-a-memoir, accessed May 17, 2017.
16. http://larrysanger.org/2004/12/why-wikipedia-must-jettison-its-anti-elitism/, accessed May 17, 2017.
17. Jim Giles, "Internet Encyclopedias Go Head to Head," *Nature*, December 14, 2005, 900–1.
18. http://en.wikipedia.org/wiki/Wikipedia:About, March 13, 2015.
19. Reagle, *Good Faith Collboration*, 3.
20. Ludwig Wittgenstein, *Tractatus Logico-Philosophicus*, ed. Ted Honderich, tr. D. F. Pears and B. F. McGuinness (London: Routledge & Kegan Paul, 1922), 7.
21. http://en.wikipedia.org/wiki/Wikipedia:About, August 12, 2016.
22. https://en.wikipedia.org/wiki/Seeing_Red_(Buffy_the_Vampire_Slayer), accessed May 17, 2017.
23. Lévi-Strauss, *The Savage Mind*, 22.
24. https://en.wikipedia.org/wiki/Wikipedia:Neutral_point_of_view, accessed May 17, 2017.
25. Thomas Nagel, *The View from Nowhere* (New York: Oxford University Press, 1986).
26. https://en.wikipedia.org/wiki/Wikipedia:Neutral_point_of_view, accessed May 17, 2017.
27. Shane Greenstein, Yuan Gu, and Feng Zhu, "Ideological Segregation among Online Collaborators: Evidence from Wikipedians," https://papers.ssrn.com/sol3/papers.cfm?abstract_id=2851934, accessed May 17, 2017.
28. https://en.wikipedia.org/wiki/Wikipedia:Protection_policy, accessed May 17, 2017.
29. https://www.bl.uk/press-releases/2015/may/cornelia-parker-unveils-13-metre-long-magna-carta-embroidery, accessed May 17, 2017.

Departments, Disciplines

The social geography of the university lays out the first region of this second chapter. So many of us talk routinely, instinctively, of the diminished scale of the academic humanities, their relative meagerness as compared to the rising ranks of professional and policy studies, or preparation for science and technology and commerce. But if the humanities are relatively small, they are absolutely numerous. Departments of philosophy or Classics or Slavic may be modest families by budgetary standards, but they remain planetary in reach. Geographically dispersed, different in emphasis, the sites of the humanities nevertheless display shared concerns voiced in comparable rooms. As you read this, they are there. And really, after all, how many of us, need there be? The humanities comprise a discontinuous multitude. I take this as their underappreciated condition—the dispersal of intellectual labor and its resources, the simultaneous pursuit of problems that meet only in conferences and footnotes. This domain, the daily world of the academic humanities, physical and social, gives the present subject. Its premise is that now more than ever we should become self-conscious of the texture of everyday routines. Thought is always embodied. Bodies move in social space. The first aim is to restore an abstraction (the humanities) to its ordinary habitat, its putter through the day.

Start by recalling the distinctive hum and rhythm of a department on a term-time Tuesday. At a fixed and early hour, the staff arrives. They will stay until the end of the day, while others come and go. Never a large body in departments of the humanities, usually between one and four, they make a social group too commonly overlooked. Low on the economic ladder of university accounting and in the table of status, much like counterparts in the corporate world, they are noticed intermittently. But by the nature of the duties, they live close to the central workings of administration. They possess delicate information, on salaries and work habits, for instance, and when sufficiently hard-pressed or just so inclined, they employ critical reason and cutting irony. Conditions are ripe for resentment, poorly recognized by fast-moving and distracted faculty. At the same time, their long hours together, while students and faculty make cameo appearances, can stir dissension. Within the indeterminacy and unpredictability of the daily round, responsibilities can be blurred: Who receives complaints from the general public? Who makes the first call for maintenance emergencies? Who reminds the faculty of the holiday party? Are the pay grades fairly drawn? Then, even in the midst of tedium and uneasiness, it's common for a long-serving staff member to be seen as the local matriarch (still almost never patriarch), justifiably praised and then sentimentally mythologized, as few others in the building ever are.

Faculty members arrive in stages, sorting themselves in degrees of obligation, purpose, and privilege. The array of obligations—to prepare a seminar, to review a manuscript, to supervise a doctoral student, to answer an outstanding email, to copy-edit an article, to send off a letter of reference by yesterday, to chair a committee, to read, to think—is various. Different aspects of temperament are summoned; there are many ways to fail; pressures are internal/external. What looks like distraction (or rudeness) is often quick scanning for the next urgency. Some, especially in the first years, are never not working: this means evenings and weekends too. Others find better rhythms, but many need a decade or two before they feel anything anyone might call "equilibrium." At the top end of a career can be found privilege and clear signs of success: respect, reputation, remuneration. Naturally, there is ample room for bitterness and jealousy here too. Then there is the natural sprawl of different understandings and practices of a vocation. Those who write for the newspapers and those who live in libraries, those who publish numerous books and those who are building to one great synthesis, those who teach famous courses and those who dread the classroom; these follow different routines, and also adopt distinct personal styles. Some tell memorable jokes, others none.

A contrast between staff and faculty on one side and students on the other is that while the first two groups are individualized—by name, title, function, and familiarity—the students are seen, and often speak of themselves, as a mass. Arriving, they place themselves around a table or in seats along rows. Intensely aware that success in the humanities calls upon their individuality, they nonetheless know that it can only show itself against the background of many others. The demand to speak up and to speak out, to become fluent, articulate, and, if possible, humorous contends with an awareness that the same speech can win a nod from the faculty and derision from student peers. To learn to be as articulate as an admired professor: this may be one pull or press. But another is not to suck up, at least not to be seen to suck up, even as you surmise that the special favor of the faculty is a good not to be scorned.

The quiet work of writing is always being practiced somewhere near. It's frequently the straightest path to success in the humanities, the capacity to mold a sentence and to adjust its tone. It can seem, and perhaps it is, a facility that can be patched and improved but never taught, something that grows in the dark or that came to be acquired through careful personal listening. Faculty (also journalists) speak abidingly of those who "can't write." But even among those who can, there are distinctions. Though the norms of good writing change through time and across cultures and subcultures, they become so embedded that they can seem eternal. Students who catch the flair and taste, who learn the norms and then learn how to give them a twist, are feted and caressed in the humanities, even talked about after hours. But writing moves along an uncertain circuit. Once praised, it might seem to deserve praise always. But the many dimensions of value in the humanities—accuracy, originality, clarity, vividness, surprise, coherence, among others—invite different judgments from different readers on different occasions. It's why there is something sadly inevitable about resentment over a grade or final mark. A student will remember success in following just this very path last term; the instructor will compare the middling effort to the others stretching before and after. Especially for young students, but in some measure for all who live by academic sentences, writing is a gift in the dark. You give it, and then you wait.

The humanities make their own dust. Even as paper gives way to bytes of light, the trooping into lecture halls and through seminar rooms leaves signs of disarray, if only in the scatter of chairs. Are humanists scruffier than the others? Probably, to some extent. Because we don't have laboratories to tend and we share common spaces in the department, we tend to be lax with coffee cups. It's a failing, then, that so little connection is made with those who clean up before and after us. They are the fourth group moving through the daily routines, and it's no good pretending that they are invited into the department community. Exceptions, of course, but years of quizzing colleagues and students— try it yourself—confirm what was expected. People have reasons for scurrying past, but beneath all, they learn to live with bad conscience. It's a failing, a stain on the humanities.

When Thought Counts

Visiting Rome after their wedding, Dorothea Casaubon (née Brooke) and her husband Edward face their first deep division. It concerns his long-standing research in world mythology. Dorothea had placed trust, love, and vision in service of the task and its fruition in a great book, *The Key to All Mythologies*. There Casaubon would demonstrate that all the world's myths "were corruptions of a tradition originally revealed." For years he has labored on his own, reading, pondering, and inscribing "a formidable range of volumes" with his notes.[1] Now in Rome, Dorothea falters in her belief. Where she hoped to find intellectual ardor, she finds desiccation, and then just as disquieting is Casaubon's reluctance to convert his knowledge into his book. He speaks of the need for further "sifting," while her worry breaks into speech:

> "And all your notes..." said Dorothea, whose heart had already burned within her on this subject, so that now she could not help speaking with her tongue. "All those rows of volumes—will you not now do what you used to speak of?—will you not make up your mind what part of them you will use, and begin to write the book which will make your vast knowledge useful to the world? I will write to your dictation."[2]

The outburst startles and angers Casaubon, who patronizes her ignorance. He cannot be distracted by the "facile conjectures of ignorant onlookers," "the impatient scorn of chatterers." But Dorothea is angry in turn. "You showed me the rows of notebooks—you have often spoken of them—you have often said that they wanted digesting. But I never heard you speak of the writing that is to be published. Those were very simple facts, and my judgment went no farther."[3] The quarrel makes a crack in brittle married harmony. It also prepares for a more shattering exchange.

Will Ladislaw, cousin to Casaubon and Dorothea's fated love, visits the Roman drawing room and finds her alone—which is just as well. For Will, Casaubon is a "dried-up pedant," an "elaborator of small explanations about as important as the surplus stock of false antiquities kept in a vendor's back chamber."[4] Unable to contain his irritation, he claims that his cousin's drudgery will "be thrown away, as so much English scholarship is, for want of knowing what is being done by the rest of the world. If Mr. Casaubon read German he would save himself a great deal of trouble." A shaken Dorothea asks to hear more. Will explains that the Germans have "taken the lead in historical inquiries, and they laugh at results which are got by groping about in woods with a pocket-compass while they have made good roads." Casaubon, has "deafened himself" against this advance in knowledge—not, the narrator qualifies, that Will himself knew what the Germans said.[5]

Brooding over these words, Dorothea frets to the end of the novel's second book, when she meets Will again and resumes the conversation. She has been thinking, she says, about the need to know German. But why? Doesn't her husband have the same materials that the German scholars study? Not exactly, Will explains, because Casaubon only has "second-hand knowledge" of recent Orientalism. And when Dorothea asks why his book couldn't stand alongside the work of past scholars "who knew nothing about these modern things," but whose work is yet read, Will replies that everything depends "on the line of study taken":

> "The subject Mr. Casaubon has chosen is as changing as chemistry: new discoveries are constantly making new points of view. Who wants a system on the basis of the four elements, or a book to refute Paracelsus? Do you not see that it is no use now to be crawling a little way after men of the last century—men like Bryant—and correcting their mistakes?—living in a lumber-room and furbishing up broken-legged theories about Chus and Mizraim?"[6]

These hard words mark a crisis in *Middlemarch*, and also a turning point in the history of knowledge. They confirm the professionalization of research that had been growing through the nineteenth century, especially on the European continent, and above all, in Germany. For George Eliot, two forces have converged. First is the emergence of systematic research with its new norms of comprehensive inquiry and collective exchange. The second is the philosophy of Auguste Comte. Knowledge, according to Comte, had passed through three long stages: religious, metaphysical, and scientific (or "positive"). Only in the nineteenth century has the final stage been reached, when the world no longer appears as the effect of supernatural forces (religion) or invisible origins (metaphysics). In the era of positivism, science abandons unseen causes (like the key to all mythologies) in favor of observed laws. Within *Middlemarch*, the other leading figure, Lydgate the doctor, follows the positivist light, challenging the superstition of village medicine, insisting on new practice guided by the latest experiment.

Casaubon belongs to no field of inquiry. He reads according to his own lights, indifferent to (because ignorant of) newer work exchanged elsewhere. Not knowing German is bad in itself. But it also stands for the wider limitation that comes from trying to astonish the world from a private corner. Casaubon's distinction—which won him the young aspiring wife—is unmasked as merely local. He is a parish celebrity of only apparent eminence, whose *Key to All Mythologies* is exposed as a crank theory. He ridicules earlier thinkers, not on the basis of established principles or agreed-upon procedures, only on the ground of his own ill-founded theories and personal crotchets.

What makes the sequence historically evocative is that it marks a moment when antiquarianism—even hard-working antiquarianism—confronts the power of a discipline. Casaubon has never seen what Dorothea has been forced to learn: that knowledge depends on emerging consensus, that it cannot be the province of lone enthusiasts, that it is perpetually changing, and that research must live up to the latest understanding (not "men of the last century"). While Dorothea hopefully reflects that her husband has the same "materials" as the Germans, Will insists both that there are materials eluding Casaubon (the "Oriental" subjects) and that his theories will be "broken-legged," that is, untested, eccentric, obsolete. Novelty is inexorable. The rector in his study misses the "new discoveries" creating "new points of view." He becomes an early figure of the pathos of independent thought, unmoored in the age of disciplines. *Middlemarch* can serve as a light-shedding parable of how canons of knowledge grow through exclusion.

Set Casaubon now against one of those who emerged from the new Germanic scholarship: Erwin Panofksy, an incarnation of the professionalization of disciplines. Beginning his career with appointments in Berlin, Munich, and Hamburg, Panofksy emigrated to the United States in the thirties. On both continents, his task was to consolidate and then extend the work of a founding generation, most notably, the work of Heinrich Wölflin. As William S. Heckscher has put it in a memoir: "In the unquestionably glorious years of the Weimar Republic, Erwin Panofsky laid the foundation of his fame as a scholar who helped to change the aesthetic and antiquarian orientation of art history and to turn it into a humanistic discipline which boldly ventured into adjacent fields."[7] The formulations are telling; so indeed are the images. "Discipline" surpasses the merely "aesthetic" and "antiquarian." The laying of a "foundation" (vertical) prepares for movement to "adjacent fields" (horizontal)—as if once a body of thought knows it can stand firmly erect, it can begin to sway from side to side. It is the motion in miniature of professionalizing humanities.

Heckscher's memoir represents not only the admiring portrait of an eminent friend but also a statement of ideal equilibrium within the disciplines of knowledge. "Panofsky's work," he writes:

> although based on genuine respect for the achievement of others—above all a wholly justified veneration of his teachers, along with a deep awareness of tradition—was nevertheless revolutionary in character. It is no exaggeration to state that almost every single one of his publications influenced the development and, more often than not, determined the direction of his chosen discipline, the history of art. He pursued his work with undiminished gusto through no less than fifty-five creative years. Conservative and radical at the same time, his oeuvre faithfully mirrors the growth of art history as a scholarly discipline.[8]

The image suggests a perfect marriage between a career and a field. The strong-willed thinker is at one with his "scholarly discipline," whose growth he develops and then mirrors. Unlike Casaubon, Panofsky's work draws upon, and therefore can contribute to, the continuous development of shared understanding. He can be both conservative and radical because he never disowns the past that he renovates. This is what "discipline" has come to mean.

In practice, if you are neither the real nor the idealized Panofsky, the relation between career and discipline is never so frictionless. Suppose we take one representative arc of an early career: a student in the middle teens feels dawning vocation in the study of art, music, or literature, in philosophy or history. We can agree that these early dawns usually shine over a (too) vast area. The first attraction is not the power of focus but the thrill of the grand view that soon can attract a still grander theory. "The Key to All Mythologies" could be the name of many essays at the beginning of the undergraduate years. A temptation endemic to the humanities, with their long histories and their call to interpretation, is that they seem open to universal thinking. Socrates and Wittgenstein, Sappho and Woolf, Rubens and Matisse can crowd into a single thought, even as the thought becomes vaporous and gauzy. Part of the impetus to the humanities is the invitation to the most capacious view. Nothing human foreign to me.

The arc of the successful career almost always requires the discovery of some particularity, indissoluble in pith and grit. But the surrender of transhistorical breathlessness doesn't come at once, and doesn't come for everyone. The caustic "too general" takes time to bite. No one, after all, begins as a specialist. The first desire, inciting, inspiring, is to read it all. Nor does this disappear, even after the arrival of professional identity—and limitation. The achievement of comprehensiveness, of sweeping knowledge, through many centuries and across the disciplines, remains a live ideal. A popular mythology of the scholar nurtures this image of "more" and "all." I met a don who knows seven languages! I met one who knows twelve! Even where the image of well-roundedness is set aside, the figure of the long-striding scholar abides. They exist. The modern history of the humanities enshrines legendary thinkers who move leapingly from China to Peru, from the pre-Socratics to postmodernism. Panofsky was one. His command of the career of Albrecht Dürer gave him the distinction of a special mastery: intricate, textured, close (*The Life and Art of Albrecht Dürer*, 1943). Alongside the focal singular came the amplitude of *Early Netherlandish Painting* (1953) and all the rolling centuries before and after: the history of visual art from the classics to Hollywood (*Meaning in the Visual Arts*, 1955). Beyond history stood canons of methodology (*Studies in Iconology*, 1939). So Northrop Frye plunged deep into the mythologies of William Blake, following lines of veiled reference and bringing private obscurities into the public light (*Fearful Symmetry*,1947). Ten years later he offered his full-scale taxonomy of literary possibility: its modes, myths, and symbols (*Anatomy of Criticism*, 1957).

The Key to All Theories, circa 1960

These last dates are pertinent, reminding us of a cresting phase of synoptic thought in the middle of the twentieth century. The lure of a total theory that preserves specificity, or of the special instance that opens to universal insight—these are legacies from Hegel that became compelling again in the mid-twentieth century and that we do well to recall here. From the early fifties, Sartre moved toward a synthesis culminating in *Search for a Method* (*Questions de méthode*, 1957), whose claim is that major systems of thought—Marxism, psychoanalysis, existentialism—can now, and must soon, complete one another. Marxism is the "unsurpassable" context that unveils the broad arc of history, but it fails to capture the singular history of an individual life. "Today's Marxists," writes Sartre,

> are concerned only with adults; reading them one would believe that we are born at the age when we earn our first wages. They have forgotten their own childhoods. As we read them, everything seems to happen as if men experienced their alienation and their reification *first in their own work*, whereas in actuality each one lives it *first*, as a child, *in his parents' work.*[9]

Psychoanalysis gives the theory of the early family agon. But it too is incomplete. The fullest theory and only adequate method must also account for the freedom-in-constraint as it is lived by individuals. This is precisely the domain of existentialism. The history of class conflict (Marxism), the struggles of family life (psychoanalysis), and the lived experience of subjectivity (existentialism) will then meet in a single method.

Sartre's project stands alongside, and competes with, the work of the Frankfurt School, which also aimed to surpass the old conflicts of interpretation. Its leading postwar thinkers—Horkheimer, Adorno, Marcuse—resisted the Sartrean defense of individuality, but were equally concerned to work out the terms of the Marx–Freud relation. Among the group, Marcuse was most disposed to systematic, even schematic solutions, unembarrassed by the grandeur of reconciliation. *Eros and Civilization* (1955) begins fearlessly, claiming that "the traditional borderlines between psychology on the one side and political and social philosophy on the other have been made obsolete by the condition of man in the present era."[10] The argument accepts the depth of the psychoanalytic insight: our lives must contend with the power of Eros and Thanatos, the instincts of life and death. But the fate of these psychic forces is not fixed and permanent. In another society, at a different historical moment, now within reach, the clash of instincts could bring about, not competition and destruction, but the free play of the senses. The "eternal" conflicts of psychoanalysis must be historicized, so that they can be disarmed and surpassed.[11] This is the lesson and urgency of theoretical reconciliation between Marx and Freud.

The third case, mid-century structuralism, shows similar ambition, but locates synthesis on a different plane. In its influential form in the writings of Lévi-Strauss, structuralism aggressively repudiated Sartre's program, denying both the priority of class history and the foundational place of consciousness. But in its own domain, it too pursued total explanation. Its task was not to move from generality to specificity, but to recognize that the general and the specific follow the same laws of structure. Language, as understood through the linguistics of Ferdinand de Saussure, offers a model for uniting social practice and human thought. A few underlying categories and concepts—the sign, metaphor and metonymy, synchronic and diachronic—govern the structure of culture across time and space. For a few years, structuralism offered itself as the most rigorous form of total explanation, one that would apply to myth and poetry, social organization, and the structure of the unconscious.

These movements, within and without academic centers, represent a time of intellectual confidence and cross-disciplinary synthesis. At a level more profound than the division of fields, it seemed possible to articulate a theory without leaks or seams. Yet at least as notable is that the flaring of these projects ended abruptly after very few years.

The proximate and near-simultaneous causes were deconstruction and feminism. The force of Derridean deconstruction was at once to annul the privilege of consciousness and to confound the coherence of structure. Founding assumptions of both Sartre and Lévi-Strauss were challenged and overturned. Claims for the centrality of consciousness were said to be trapped in bottomless self-contradiction; the terms that governed structuralism (signified and signifier, speech and writing) were seen as unstable and mutually corrosive. Near-simultaneously, a theoretically and politically enlivened feminism challenged the exclusions of the Marx–Freud synthesis. Where were women in the system of containers that enclosed the individual within the family within the class? What could it mean to overcome the separation of social and psychological categories without taking gender into account? The demand was to unravel the seamlessness of Capital-plus-Oedipus and to recognize a feminist theory that went as deep as instinct or class. From the later sixties onward, any movement toward "total theory" has faced ready charges of incoherence or partiality.

Systematic approaches haven't disappeared from the humanities. But within the broader arc of the last three decades, their pre-eminence has been lost, both in the training of doctoral students and in leading programs of research. The metaphor of "lens" has become pervasive and also perhaps symptomatic. Any idle lunchtime search for the phrase "through the lens of" can carry you quickly past coffee. The lens of power, of discourse analysis, the lenses of nostalgia and intertexuality, the lens of a more primordial phenomenological truth. What it carries, this figure of the lens, is a double connotation of portability and pragmatism. A lens is not itself a full-blown theory but a provisional way of seeing. It remains external to the thinker; it's not a conviction or a commitment; it's a lens. As such, it can be altered or abandoned (or used again). It is anything but totalizing. The phrase "through the lens of" admits that other lenses would bring other landscapes into different focus.

Broadly speaking (that is, through a lens with wide focus), we can recognize this historical divergence as our inheritance in the new millennium. The synthesis that seemed possible, even imminent, sixty years ago remains a regulative ideal for many scholars: a consistency of method, a rigor that can be called scientific, governed by an articulate theory and often an aspiration toward the unity of disciplines. Such research may not attain a final truth in its domain, but it can be so extensive as to seem nearly exhaustive. Opposing the ambition of such views stands a radical perspectivism that, openly or implicitly, acknowledges that many lenses will yield many views and that no superior "lens" will enlarge to the unity of interpretation. Now (2017), at a moment when the second paradigm is ascendant, the goals of the first can seem speculative, quaint, implausible from the start. But a better approach to the history is to see it as still unfolding. The assertions of "theoretical unity" and "illuminating perspective" are poles within which the humanities have moved during the last hundred years: at telling moments, one has corrected the other. Claims of deep definitive explanation (as in Sartre's studies of Genet and Flaubert) come to seem loose, baggy, and vulnerable, even surprisingly so. But what's called "speculative" will appear "rigorous" or even "self-evident" when norms are shared. Such norms may come again. We live within a history of recent thought which moves between times when synthetic claims seem warranted and those when chastened thought retreats to safe particulars. Historians often see literary criticism as too "hypothetical," while the critics may call historians unduly "cautious."

In the last two years, the contrast has sharpened again, this time from within the discipline of history itself. *The History Manifesto* (Jo Guldi and David Armitage, 2014) offers an urgent rebuttal of the drift toward "the Short Past," a turn in research toward "shorter and shorter time-scales and more and more intensive use of archives."[12] Since the 1970s, runs the thought, history has lost the inspiration of Fernand Braudel's *longue durée* stretching over many centuries, and has retreated to views of a few decades or less. The narrow specialization can be seen to offer some professional advantages:

> A generation with limited prospects on the jobmarket increasingly defined itself by its mastery of discrete archives...Exploiting archives became a coming-of-age ritual for a historian, one of the primary signs by which one identified disciplined commitment to methodology, theoretical sophistication, a saturation in historiographical context, and a familiarity with documents.[13]

The unfortunate result has been a loss of the social consequence of historical writing. Undue intellectual modesty has kept history from meeting its responsibility, not only to deeper understanding of the past, but also to current policy debates that must draw on long temporal awareness. Deep historians, says *The History Manifesto*, are best suited to nurturing our thinking about the future.

The book generated strong immediate reaction, partly in praise, but partly in fierce repudiation. The decision to publish the work online with open access, the authors' use of social media to promote, extend, and defend their arguments, and the general stir of interest led the *American Historical Review* to break with its usual practice and to lay out the terms of contention without requiring ordinary peer review. The *AHR* accepted the offer of Deborah Cohen and Peter Mandler to present a (radical and withering) critique, followed by a response from Guldi and Armitage. Cohen and Mandler reject the enabling assumption of the *Manifesto* (that historians ever made a turn to the Short Past) and all that is claimed to follow:

> When the underpinnings of their manifesto are examined, the supporting evidence either is nonexistent or mandates just the opposite conclusion. This is true for each of their major propositions: the retreat of the *longue durée* they posit, the correlation they draw between the length of time a study covers and its significance, the alleged salience of long-term arguments to policymaking, the presumptions about historians' superiority as arbiters of big data, and the crisis of the humanities that requires the cure they are proposing.[14]

Guldi and Armitage retort to this "vigorous response"[15] by charging that it represents "an apology for business as usual and a defense of the status quo."[16] They acknowledge, as they do in the *Manifesto*, that micro history has power and urgency, but then reiterate the "greater danger in going too short rather than too long."[17] The dispute has a dispiriting edginess to it, but it captures agitations that can be productive if they don't depress you too badly. The issues, after all, are substantial. How do disciplines change? What are the wider effects of the research, both for the health of a discipline and for life outside the university? How much has been altered by the new technologies?

Almost everything? Quite a lot? Or some? Is there a "crisis" in the humanities? (More on this later.)

For our purposes here, the pressing question concerns the reach and limitation of research. Guldi and Armitage emphasize the professionalizing advantages of the specialist archive (a "coming-of-age ritual"), which no doubt plays a role. But in fact, the twentieth-century history of the humanities, in one form or another, experienced repeated reactions to the too vast, the too sweeping, too thin and reductive. An early movement was the refusal of metaphysics in the philosophic revolution led by Frege, Russell, Moore, and Wittgenstein. But in less technical terms, many adjacent disciplines shared a suspicion of large-scale systems of thought. The rise of modern professionalism was often seen as a reaction to late nineteenth-century intellectual shallowness: grand but impressionistic, far-reaching but ungrounded, too abstract even to refute. To professionalize was thus often to particularize. Throughout the century, a central task of critique has been to expose the vulnerability of over-general syntheses; this is surely one reason that even the brilliance of total theory in the hands of Lévi-Strauss or Sartre was so susceptible to rapid dismantling.

The issue recurs with a vengeance in the controversies around *The History Manifesto*. The main thrust of their book, say Guldi and Armitage, was:

> to affirm the greater possibilities that are now emerging for writing such extensive histories earlier rather than later in historians' careers. The aim was accordingly not to constrain ambition but to encourage it, and not to truncate historical inquiries—particularly by younger researchers—when they require pursuit over larger expanses of time or space.[18]

The question of the Long and the Short differs, of course, from the contest between total theory and the lens, but they are similar in their differences. They meet vividly during job interviews with the young scholar, where a candidate must defend both the sharp focus of the research project and a wide range of interests. Guldi and Armitage are solicitous toward the demands on an early career driven toward topics of short duration and toward a determinate method and theory. But by the nature of the lifespan and doctoral training, the successful candidate is always likely to be relatively particular and distinctly specialized, even if traversing many decades (or centuries) and even if sophisticated in theory.

Departments in Disciplines, Disciplines in Departments

Here is where disciplines and departments come into difficult but also revealing conflict. Especially in the last third of the twentieth century, disciplines have widened their domains and dramatically expanded the objects and events they study. Younger scholars are needed to define these emerging areas. During this same period, methodology has become self-conscious, technical, and varied, placing increasing strain on shared practice within each field. The excavation of new subjects and the articulation of new methods—these disciplinary conditions, exciting if formidable, create strains for the institutional life of departments. Disciplines develop sub-fields in profusion; departments seek to maintain coverage of areas appropriate to their high standing and to the training of doctoral students. At the same time, resistance to duplicated expertise is an institutional reflex, reinforced by budgets outstripped by the subfields. Certain large figures and texts—Dante, Kant, Woolf, Da Vinci, the Bible—may still be the special emphases of more than one professor, but the prospect of having two dedicated Spenserians will seem a pleasure too expensive to murmur. The differential character of humanities' departments—a wariness of replication and unquenchable desire for more coverage—is pronounced. "We already have our colleague Claxon holding down the baroque, while we don't have anyone serious about Debussy or Sibelius": this is not only a familiar style of utterance; it also marks the place where intellectual and institutional burdens meet.

At the time of appointment, especially of young scholars to first positions, the stresses show themselves. At research universities, an embarrassing gap in a specialized area is a dominant concern. But within a buyer's market, the searchers can be choosy. Dazzlingly clever intellects can be found, who fit the specialized bill, and have established achievements to confirm it. Sooner or later, though, in both interviews and later deliberations, the question of teaching arises. Now the issue is whether the candidate can meet a variety of assignments, spanning centuries, problems, forms, etc. Even as successful research tends toward a specialized area, new or badly needed, the associated teaching tends to fall within existing structures of the department's curriculum and inevitably will be broader than the research area. Furthermore, pressures on department size only increase the separation between broad responsibilities in the lecture hall and the specificities of research.

The season of hiring exposes departments to the instability of existing arrangements and even enabling assumptions. It appears in the uncertainty of historically organized departments (Art History, English, Music) toward the dominance of "period thinking" at the expense of other ways (by genre or topic, for instance) of articulating their subjects. It occurs in debates within religious studies as to whether the field has something as determinate as a framing subject matter. And it enters philosophy when a male-dominated discipline not only attempts to include (and promote) female colleagues but also to accept gender as a substantive area of research and teaching. Because the quarter-century after World War II saw rapid expansion in the scale of higher education—more students educated, more faculty members needed, more universities built—departmental memory retains nostalgic images of near-full coverage with prospects for still more. Given persisting frameworks formed at the time of abundance, it's easy to grasp the uneasy self-understanding that erupts in faculty meetings. A department that owes its reputation to three distinguished medievalists of a generation ago will struggle to find principles helping it to decide whether to trim to one position or to launch a bloody fight to sustain two—at least!

A study from the Carnegie Foundation on the future of doctoral education named its focus in a subtitle: "Stewards of the Discipline." A "steward" is a scholar "who will creatively generate new knowledge, critically conserve valuable and useful ideas, and responsibly transform those understandings through writing, teaching, and application."[19] Carnegie invited leading figures from many disciplines to reflect on this theme, but it also noted that "Not only do we focus on disciplines but within disciplines we assume that the key educational community is the academic department—the nexus of the discipline and the institution."[20] Here is the anodyne view, the department as tactical mediator, tending the "nexus." Yet in the humanities, and often beyond, departments struggle to define the disciplines they represent, relying on formulations too abstract to capture the many tasks sheltered beneath the department umbrella. Creative work, digital analysis, inter-media relations, the editing of journals, the preservation of materials, the directing of institutes, history, theory, interpretation—versions of these and other activities occupy most humanities departments. What can be gained by dragooning them into discipline, when they represent many disciplines, often opaque to one another? Far from being a "nexus" between discipline and institution, departments are weakly bounded zones of intellectual work, traversed by widely varying interests, which resist stable articulation.

Departments and disciplines cannot be expected to achieve enduring equilibrium, and the imbalance between them is an everyday vexation. Deliberation and dispute over curriculum, governance, and hiring appear regularly and consequentially. As fields grow through the articulation of subfields and new topics, through new developments in theory and the urgent demand to diversify, departments can endure legendary struggle to reach common ground, or even a clarifying vote, on their future direction. Then, too, the willingness to gauge opinion widely—among the youngest faculty and also doctoral students—makes generational differences visible, even if they are rarely fully aired.

*

A department, in or out of the humanities, is a churning microsociety, which ought to become more interesting to its citizens. Its discipline and sub-disciplines orient it toward novelty, toward original contributions to knowledge. But department membership changes slowly. Arrivals and departures, charged as these events can be, do little to disrupt the prevailing continuity of embedded culture. The contrast between fast-moving fields and slow-changing communities always risks unstable deliberation. As new fields develop (Global History, Digital Humanities, African-American and Asian-American studies), it's often a small minority that recognizes the emergent thought. It may well be that no one in the department has had formal training or even sustained encounter with the area. A few, especially those who take responsibility for staying "current," must make the case to the larger group. Skepticism, always appropriate to some point, can seem retrograde and exasperating beyond that point.

The theory conflicts at the end of the last millennium gave spectacular display to a conflict that may be no less consequential when it is quietly chronic. The division can be, and can be cast as, generational or ideological, merely personal or systematically political. One side speaks of "faddists," the other of "old farts." These smaller anecdote-inciting aspects of everyday life should not be overlooked. After all, it's not simply that research in the humanities tends to be individualizing; the daily round of work and reward continually separates the members of the faculty from one another. We rarely see the classroom teaching of more than a few of our colleagues and are likely to know little of locally generated scholarship beyond that of those in the same or nearby fields. Personal traits—eccentricity, amiability, jealousy, benevolence—are probably no more significant than in any other office environment. But the elusive grounds of reward, from salary to promotion to prize-winning, can create unsettling effects within the individualizing districts of the humanities. Achievements are in one sense nearly incommensurable: the editor of sacred texts and the anthropologically inspired scholar of new ritual practices in Russia may have neighboring offices while belonging to vastly different universes of discourse. But because they are neighbors on the same corridor, they also witness their fully commensurable conditions: the number of students forming a line outside the office, the work on committees, the appearance or non-appearance at visiting lectures. Moreover, these acts of comparison are frequently long-lived. Faculty members are aging together, and as individual caretakers of their own careers, who are also regularly visible to each other, the opportunities are rife for resentment, self-assertion, and self-justification. It doesn't require deep ethnography to recognize the intricate cross-cutting ambitions and dispositions that make planning from above—from the perch of provost or dean—so liable to end in exasperation.

Impatient proposals for reform often issue in persuasive, well-motivated advice. In the Carnegie study, you find these spiky words from the historian Thomas Bender: "Mentoring of doctoral students . . . needs ventilating. Although a principal adviser is essential in doctoral education, the culture of the department must encourage more open relationships and sustain a plurality of significant advisers at all stages of graduate education."[21] The language of "must" and "need" reappears throughout the long volume and comes to crescendo in the final essay by George E. Walker, which heightens the tone of urgency:

> We must be willing to relinquish some old habits and ways of mind. We need a collective will. We need to accept our shared responsibility to engage in this process. And we need to act with strong leadership and an understanding of the need for change. The power of our vision for doctoral education can help sustain us and should provide the impetus for creative problem solving.[22]

Perhaps. But within these elevated tones one hears the echo of an earlier contribution, David Damrosch's, which offered more rueful thoughts on the prospects for change:

> With virtual unanimity, our essayists praise the growth of inter-disciplinary work and discuss the need to find a new balance of disciplinary rigor and cross-disciplinary breadth; they promote the value of team teaching, and they advance ideas for new sorts of collaborative work, whether in labs or on dissertations.... Yet the very similarity of many proposals in essay after essay is depressing as well: if everybody knows what needs to be done, why are so few programs doing it.[23]

Damrosch wryly notes that "we academics are better placed to solve the world's problems than our own. It is hard to get analytical purchase on the situation in which we are immersed."[24]

If we know what to do but don't get it done, the problem is not, chiefly, weakness of will, poor leadership, personal stubbornness, or even principled resistance. All these play a part. But the difficult fact, as the Carnegie volume inadvertently shows, is that historical and institutional circumstances make change difficult and erratic. If faculty fail to achieve "analytical purchase" on themselves, this is not because their membership is unreflective, or unfriendly to analysis. Surely, it's because the object—academic departmentality—is complex and elusive, the medium in which faculty and students move without being a subject of intellectual focus. The life of the department is open to rounds of gossip, rumor, joke, and bickering, but it is not well suited for sustained self-analysis. Its preoccupations are usually separate and serial: a new appointment, a change in requirements for the doctoral exam, the report of the diversity committee. Novelty can expose the patched-together incoherence that we train ourselves not to notice.

Take the case of Environmental Humanities. Supported by the Mellon Foundation, my university initiated a series of appointments in this new area, which was taken to epitomize the virtues of interdisciplinary research. Two lessons can be drawn from the venture. First, with little history, no consensus of method, and few scholarly paradigms, the field brought widely different futures to mind. Departments were invited to collaborate on proposals for the new appointments, with the search led by a cross-department committee. The result was that the concept of an Environmental Humanities came in every dimension. Some emphasized the thematic power of landscape in cultural artifacts; some stressed the human costs of development; others took up the ethical foundations of climate activism. The local outcomes were happy. Strong appointments were made; departments extended their reach; the curriculum received some jolt. But, within the frame of the grant, the intellectual unclarity was unrelieved. Environmental Humanities was a welcome invitation to original thought, but it offered precious little in the way of foundational assumptions, shared techniques, or a common terminology. Nothing is gained by calling it an emerging discipline. Even the more flexible reach of "field" is challenged by the blooming diversity of concerns offered under the benign name.

Because two (and, in principle, three) departments joined to sponsor the appointments, the question of review and promotion arose early. Here is the second lesson taught by the Mellon initiative. The higher committee exchanged memories of contentious and career-ending deliberations, when a candidate for promotion faced review from more than one department. Needs, values, and histories failed to coincide, as who should have doubted? A young scholar required to meet standards of quite different intellectual milieux— philosophy and art history, or media studies and English—may end by facing mutually uncomprehending evaluators, whose dissonance can be the undoing of a career. Yes, a brilliant mind may crack the code and appeal to all comers. But even brilliance has to contend with not just contrasting but even incommensurable standards of achievement.

Our solution was to identify a "tenure home" for each appointment, designating just one of the participating departments as the site of evaluation. The other(s) would join the relevant committees and appear at the time of deliberation. But the determining voice and decisive majority reside with the single department, the tenure home. It's a practical solution to an intellectual impasse, and it captures the difficulties beneath the smiling calls to interdisciplinarity. It's easy enough to name an area, much harder to discover common practices aligned beneath the name. The sheer diversity of projects under Environmental Humanities should be expected: this is what happens when broad domains of knowledge are brought together and novelty is invited to occupy their intersection. We ought to have expected that notions of novelty would be unsettled and ill-defined and that systems of evaluation would clash.

Ranking, Rating: The Humanities Enumerated

Then there is evaluation on the grander scale. Beyond the department stand upper administrators, boards of accreditation, world rankings, league tables, and the REF. This last, the Research Excellence Framework, is the recent British incarnation of a program of national assessment that began in the eighties and has passed through substantial revision since then. Its stated aims are revealingly various. The goals are to assess the quality of research; to provide benchmarks for international comparison; to use the evaluation as basis for the allocation of research support; to promote diversity and equality. No British reader needs to be told that the controversies are myriad, ongoing, unresolved, and unavailing.

Derek Sayer, historian, composed a much-noticed polemic (*Rank Hypocrisies*) against the REF in 2014. The curt terms of critique are tallied early:

> [the] narrow disciplinary remit of REF panels and their inability to evaluate interdisciplinary research, the inconsistencies of using nationally recruited panels to make judgments of comparative international excellence, the risks of replication of entrenched academic hierarchies and networks inherent in HEFCE's procedures for appointment of panel members, the unrealistic

volume of work expected of panelists, the perversity of excluding all external indicators of quality from assessments, and the incompetence of REF panels to provide sufficient diversity and depth of expertise to evaluate the outputs that fall under their remit.[25]

Each of the claims opens to pointed, useful conversation, but my pressing concern is the uneasy place of the humanities within the systems of appraisal. Since publication of the 2014 REF, other reports have appeared. Though their tone is more cautious than Sayer's, the murmur of critique is unceasing.

James Wilsdon, professor of Science and Democracy at the University of Sussex, chaired a group convened by HEFCE to evaluate the evaluation. Title and subtitle together—"The Metric Tide: Report of the Independent Review of the Role of Metrics in Research Assessment and Management"—neatly (or, rather, clumsily) condense the mix of trope and bureaucratese. The title means to evoke King Canute before the onrushing waves, because like Canute's sea, "The metric tide is rising." So, for instance, citation counting remains coin of the assessment realm, but how and what to count? The favored markers are DOIs ("Digital Object Indicators," didn't you know?) but the committee is clear that they are "not sufficient for robust metrics."[26] A better protocol, more journal-sensitive, would allow the REF to ask, for instance, "How many articles has a particular author produced with citations above the average for the journal in question?" Even so, the problem will remain that "Use of DOIs varies by discipline, and is still less common in the arts and humanities than in other areas."[27] Largely, this is because citations in the humanities are predominantly within books citing other books, but books are not captured at all adequately within SCOPUS. "The Metric Tide" retreats to plausibility: "Expert peer judgment of books seems to be by far the best method but it is even more time-consuming and expensive than article peer assessment because books are generally much longer. In response, alternative sources have been investigated for book impact assessment, including syllabus mentions, library holding counts, book reviews, and publisher prestige."[28]

The quantitative tangle is dense; it grows denser in another recently commissioned study, "A Review of the UK's Interdisciplinary Research using a Citation-Based Approach: Report to the UK HE funding bodies and MRC by Elsevier" (July 2015). Forgive my insistence on your reading its statement of method:

We use a citation-based approach to identify IDR and measure interdisciplinarity. The basic principle behind our approach is that, if an article cites papers that are "far away" from each other in terms of their topics, it is likely to be interdisciplinary. Otherwise, it is likely to be a monodisciplinary article. Our measure of IDR is a score based only on the research output and does not take into consideration the underlying processes of knowledge integration in cross-discipline research.

The advantage of our approach is the lack of reliance on any pre-defined subject classification to define interdisciplinarity, and is flexible enough to capture the dynamics of the research landscape in which subjects are constantly emerging and changing. We however also recognise the limitations of the approach when looking at a subset of the research outputs produced by the UK, in particular the publications in the research domain of the Humanities.[29]

The image of the "far away" relation appears in another Elsevier publication (see Figure 1).

Figure 1 Five-Year Journal Map: Elsevier Mapping Interdisciplinary Research.

George Lan, Sophia Katrenko, and Lei Pan, *Analyzing Interdisciplinary Research along Multiple Dimensions of Research Impact*. ASIS&T 2015 Metrics Workshop November 7, 2015.

The failure to capture (inter)disciplinary relations in two-dimensional space is painfully evident. Conspicuous too is the absence of the humanities, unsurprising in light of the report's concession that its methodology "may limit the ability of the approach to give a comprehensive view of IDR [interdisciplinary research] in the Humanities, and the results on the Humanities in this report require cautious interpretation."[30] You don't say.

The humanities (and humanistic social sciences) are the problem children for metric management. Sometimes, as just above, the implication is that, with more time and added bytes, they can be appraised along the same lines as the sciences. But in too many other sentences, acknowledgment is made of a recalcitrance embedded in the nature of the research itself. Projects in the humanities often take many years, extending beyond the five-year window for submission of "outputs"; they emanate from a culture of originality that places strain on peer review; they take the shape of books which resist digital processing and require time-consuming evaluation. Pondering these and other difficulties, *The Metric Tide* draws the bland moral, which has somehow grown sparky in these times: "Some of the most precious qualities of academic culture resist simple quantification, and individual indicators can struggle to do justice to the richness and plurality of our research."[31] The measured tones cannot quite mute the years of resentment, noisy and whispered.

The weight of assessment will not soon melt away. It's right to resist it more strenuously—to resist the crudeness of measure, the time-draining bureaucracy of review, the power of the upper hierarchies. No more than religious faith, romantic love, or moral conscience should higher education be strictly evaluated in market terms, certified by peer review, or required to justify itself by quantitative measure. Measure can be harmless and helpful. Surely, we want to know the demographic profile of undergraduates, the employment history of postgraduates, and to heed surveys of student reaction to their university experience. But the extension of measure into domains where it cannot count accurately—the importance or impact of scholarly research—is one of the great category mistakes of our time. This is where the humanities can again serve as figure for all liberal studies. Its successes exist in multiple dimensions of time, of geographical reach, of intellectual influence (delayed or immediate), of personal and public consequence. Like religion, which we should keep as close counterpart, the humanities represent long-standing practices that will always be open to challenge and critique, but that should vigorously resist simplifying measurements distorting the many-sided experience of vocation.

Yet, because market models and quantitative assessment have encroached upon the universities, undeterred by their category mistakes, it's not hard to find more distortions gathering in everyday academic life—unless, that is, you sidle to your office with eyes downcast. The most damaging is the degradation of academic labor through the use of ill-paid adjunct faculty, who often receive no benefits, no prospects, and no respect. In the United States, the dwindling of tenure-track positions and the spread of adjunct labor is extensive and well documented. Elsewhere, it's been less a matter of rapid degradation and more the perpetuation of hierarchies of status, pay, and privilege. The recent edifying focus has been the conflict over graduate student labor. Administrators and many professors have held that, as apprentices within a system of training, the students are not laborers but mentees, who teach as part of their advanced education. But as has become bitingly clear, only a diminishing number of graduate students will secure tenure-track appointments, and many will work outside the university. It has become implausible and self-serving to keep up the language of apprenticeship.

In the summer of 2016, in response to a case at Columbia University, the National Labor Relations Board ruled that graduate students at private universities in the U.S. have the right to unionize. As I write, students at several universities are scheduling votes on whether to join unions. The same crystalizing arguments recur. University administration typically holds that unionization would disrupt the goals of education, and that collective bargaining is at odds with the individualist character of the student–faculty relationship. On their side, the graduate organizers point to the changing character of the university, its entanglement with corporate models (and with corporations). The view here (that is, my view) is that unionization is long overdue, unworrying (as comparative studies have suggested), and well justified.

The damage to the university, heavily borne by the adjunct staff and less directly by all others, has been veiled by the power of vocation. The opportunity to land a good faculty position and to lead a life committed to inquiry remains powerfully attractive—ever more remote, but not yet impossible. Doctoral students subsist with low-level work, while waiting for another year to pass before the next round of jobs is advertised. Adjunct faculty notice their disproportionate teaching burdens and also notice the tenured faculty not noticing. What creates aggravation and bad conscience is that the satisfactions of the task, if they can be disentangled from the corrosions around them, endure. The testimony of even the most disadvantaged is ringingly clear: the work is important, increasingly urgent, and fulfilling. If even minimal standards of security, status, and pay were secure, the life commitment would be acceptable—more than acceptable, valuable.

The "Trouble of Thinking"

I deplore charges of sentimentality or self-deception, freely cast whenever demands to improve the university are made, as if the effort to preserve the independent vocation of knowledge were naive and obsolete. In fact, it remains our best chance: to let universities work according to their own best lights and, in so doing, to let them contribute to social flourishing. What, after all, is more sentimental than belief in the magic cure of quantities, efficiencies, and markets? The difficulty of getting purchase on the community of knowledge, its micro-sociology, obstructs clear thinking about useful change that is significant and near. A step forward must be the drawing of more detailed pictures of the concrete and varied existence out of which the humanities emerge. Then a longer step can be taken by considering how this community lives through time.

In this task, it will be important not to be embarrassed by a return to first principles and historical precedents. But one aspect of our resistance must be to carry on regardless. Carrying on includes all these routines of the daily humanities, and one other, on which this chapter will conclude: namely, the act of thought. It too is part of the regular everyday round. It can even claim to be its essence. But is there anything more difficult to think about than thought itself; whence it comes and where it goes; how it can be slow and tangled, but also clean and wide and bright; how there might be more of it; how it can know itself as new and meaningful; how it *is*?

The recent campaign for "critical thinking" is worthy but vague. Its central demands are incontestable: respect for evidence, suspicion of fluent rhetoric, detachment from dogma, the refusal to accept truth without inspection and questioning. But the slogan has become an edge blunted by virtue. Here is a characteristic statement:

> Critical thinking is the intellectually disciplined process of actively and skillfully conceptualizing, applying, analyzing, synthesizing, and/or evaluating information gathered from, or generated by, observation, experience, reflection, reasoning, or communication, as a guide to belief and action. In its exemplary form, it is based on universal intellectual values that transcend subject matter divisions: clarity, accuracy, precision, consistency, relevance, sound evidence, good reasons, depth, breadth, and fairness.[32]

No one can exactly oppose this program, but neither can anyone visualize it. It's true that, in the university and beyond, many offend against the canons of evidence, consistency, and clarity; Orwell's warnings remain urgent; it's right to unmask errors in logic, weakness of evidence, and the perplexities of cause and correlation. But in real ways, the parade of unexceptional virtues distracts from the more difficult and pressing issue: not critical thinking, but thinking as such.

An extreme but enlightening case is that of Wittgenstein at the moment of his publishing of the *Philosophical Investigations*. Its thoughts, he writes in a short preface, are the "precipitate" of sixteen years of reflection, which ended in admission that he could never "weld my results together into such a whole." Long-meditated ideas must be left as "philosophic remarks" because it could never do "to force them on in any single direction against their natural inclinations." The result is an "album" that Wittgenstein had doubted he could ever publish in his lifetime. But as his ideas circulated in typescripts and conversations and then came back to him, the misrepresentations "stung [his] vanity." During the same period, he reread his first great work, the *Tractatus Logico-Philosophicus*, recognizing how thoroughly his views had changed. These stray circumstances finally prodded him to complete the *Investigations*, even as he harbored doubts about its quality, which he feels incapable of improving. It's "not impossible," though unlikely, that the book will cast some light "into one brain or another."[33] So he publishes after all.

Extreme but enlightening, because even by the lesser lights of later minds, thought follows some twisting course like this. It may not take sixteen years to complete the task, but it always seems to take longer than it should. When Wittgenstein speaks of not forcing the "natural inclination" of his thoughts,[34] he evokes an elusive but commonly noted experience, the perception that thoughts assume a necessity of their own, as if, once thought, they seem to come from somewhere else. It's the drama of living up to what one has oneself conceived, a task which has a purity and integrity, even as it mixes with the lower motives of "vanity." His short preface is its own album, the testimony of exhausted thought remembering its fits, starts, satisfactions, regrets, and settlements. "I should not like my writing to spare other people the trouble of thinking," he concludes, and the phrase is priceless.[35] The "trouble of thinking" is a fit name for the humanities.

"Every six weeks," remarked Panofksy, "I have a thought. The rest of the time I work."[36] For Panofksy, as for Wittgenstein, time is always in question, the time found for thought and the time it takes to think. If any of our books were read aloud continuously, they would finish in a weekend. Why, then, does it take years to find all the words, to tune their sound, and to find the right pitch of ideas? Partly, the answer is that for thought to grow outwards, it must also curve back on itself, looking down the stem, peering into the thick hedgerow, down to its roots.

The achievements of solitary research—idea, lecture, essay, book—have come under too hasty critique from the cheerleaders for collaboration and interdisciplinarity. The brain is another discontinuous multitude. Many of its successes are bound to arrive one mind at a time. We do want, I do want, more collaboration in all aspects of our work, but the demand can become too pious when it ignores the lonely work performed one consciousness at a time. Within the fraught imperfections of the university, thought opens when and where it can. Before it crystallizes in a book, essay, or sentence, long before it becomes an "output," an idea is a looping string of concentration, held fast for a moment while another loop extends, then dropped when the tangle becomes too great, only to be knotted and reknotted in arduous intermittent labor. That moment in Panofsky's six weeks when he thinks, or thought arises or descends, is as unpredictable as it is precious. Do we really want to harry and press it to become a digit in a metric?

Notes

1. George Eliot, *Middlemarch*, ed. David Carroll (Oxford: Oxford University Press, 1988), Book I, ch. 3.
2. Ibid., Book II, ch. 20.
3. Ibid.
4. Ibid., Book II, ch. 21.
5. Ibid.
6. Ibid., Book II, ch. 22.
7. William S. Heckscher, "Erwin Panofsky: A Curriculum Vitae," in Irving Lavin, ed., *Three Essays on Style* (Cambridge, MA: MIT Press, 1995), 181.
8. Ibid., 172.
9. Jean-Paul Sartre, *Search for a Method* (New York: Random House, 1963), 62.
10. Herbert Marcuse, *Eros and Civilization: A Philosophical Inquiry into Freud* (Boston, MA: Beacon Press, 1955), 1.
11. Robert Young, "The Naked Marx," *New Statesman*, 78 (7 November 1969): 666–7.
12. Jo Guldi and David Armitage, *The History Manifesto* (Cambridge: Cambridge University Press, 2014), 46.
13. Ibid., 42, 44.
14. Deborah Cohen and Peter Mandler, "*The History Manifesto*: A Critique," *American Historical Review*, 120, 2 (April 2015): 530.
15. David Armitage and Jo Guldi, "*The History Manifesto*: A Reply to Deborah Cohen and Peter Mandler," *American Historical Review*, 120, 2 (April 2015): 544.
16. Ibid., 545.
17. Ibid., 549.
18. Ibid.
19. Chris M. Golde, "Preparing Stewards of the Discipline," in Chris M. Golde and George E. Walker, eds., *Envisioning the Future of Doctoral Education: Preparing Stewards of the Discipline* (San Francisco: Jossey-Bass, 2006), 5.
20. Ibid., 8.
21. Thomas Bender, "Expanding the Domain of History," in Golde and Walker, eds., *Envisioning the Future*, 305.
22. George E. Walker, "The Questions in the Back of the Book," in Golde and Walker, eds., *Envisioning the Future*, 427.
23. David Damrosch, "Vectors of Change," in Golde and Walker, eds., *Envisioning the Future*, 34.
24. Ibid., 35.
25. Derek Sayer, *Rank Hypocrisies: The Insult of the REF* (London: Sage Publications, 2015), 3.
26. James Wilsdon et al., *The Metric Tide: Report of the Independent Review of the Role of Metrics in Research Assessment and Management*. DOI: 10.13140/RG.2.1.4929.1363.
27. Ibid.

28. Ibid., 44.
29. Lei Pan and Sophia Katrenko, *A Review of the UK's Interdisciplinary Research using a Citation-based Approach: Report to the UK HE Funding Bodies and MRC by Elsevier*, http://www.hefce.ac.uk/pubs/rereports/Year/2015/interdisc/Title,104883,en.html, 2.
30. Ibid., 12.
31. Ibid., 2.
32. Michael Scriven and Richard Paul, "A statement presented at the 8th Annual International Conference on Critical Thinking and Education Reform," http://www.criticalthinking.org/pages/critical-thinking-where-to-begin/796.
33. Ludwig Wittgenstein, *Philosophical Investigations*, ed. G. E. M. Anscombe (Oxford: Blackwell, 1953), Preface, ix–x.
34. Ibid., Preface, ix.
35. Ibid., Preface, x.
36. Heckscher, *Three Essays on Style*, 174.

3

Experts and Expertise

"The man does not exist who, outside his own specialty, is not credulous."

Borges, "The Secret Miracle"[1]

In the weeks just before the 2016 UK referendum on continued membership in the European Union, the Tory politician Michael Gove provided one of the signature remarks of the campaign. "I think," said Gove, "that people in this country are tired of experts."[2] It took little time for the thought (and tone) to resonate widely, as an index of national, but also global populism aggressively refusing elite consensus. Politicians and press feasted on the comment. Though often defended, it was also seen as a celebration of ignorance and prejudice, a willful denial of the hierarchy of knowledge on which modern policymaking depends. What Gove went on to say was less widely reported. In place of the authority of experts, he offered the persuasiveness of arguments, forms of reasoning available to all voters, independent of their credentials. At the end of the year, he elaborated: "I think the right response in a democracy to assertions made by experts is to say 'show us the evidence, show us the facts'."[3] Another less visible comment extends the frame and helps to define the issue. In response to the Charlie Hebdo killings of 2015, Martin Wolf, economic columnist for the *Financial Times*, asked, "What is to be done? I claim no expertise in this area. But I claim at least an interest: that of a citizen of a liberal democracy, which I very much wish to remain."[4] Between the two remarks stretches an ill-marked patch of implication that lays out the concern of this chapter: the field of the expert and the claims of expertise. The discussion will move steadily toward the question of expertise in the humanities, but the issue demands a variety of perspectives and wide contexts.

Well before the debates over Brexit, Brian Wynne had described the "reflexive processes of late modernity in which expertise is widely and openly contested."[5] Within the fields of history and philosophy of science in which Wynne works, the insight is now a commonplace. From the effects of Chernobyl to silicone breast implants, from global warming to free trade, controversy over policy has become inseparable from the legitimacy of expert judgment. The politics of the contending positions, moreover, are far from stable; attacks on elite expertise are made from the right and the left. Conservative politicians work to subvert the authority of climate scientists, while left activists undermine the domination of orthodox economics.

Much of the force of expertise, its concept and its sociology, lies in images of fewness. Pictures of a pyramid are always near. At the bottom stands ignorance; competence occupies a broad middle; and the summit belongs to the experts alone. The reigning assumption is that a system of credentials has entitled the expert to authoritative judgment, which can now be trusted under the radiance of the name. Worries about elites are unavoidable where fewness is concerned, but the class of experts may be the most durable of the privileged social positions within contemporary society. Wealth and power can come and go (though now perhaps more in principle than in practice), while the peculiar feature of expertise is that, once assigned and achieved, it tends to persist as permanent endowment. Having been fully credentialed in the modeling of economic growth or the texts of *Piers Plowman*, the standing is often retained, even after successful challengers have risen in the field. Experts are more often surrounded by other younger experts than they are dethroned.

Their "fewness" lends them a mystique, but it also raises suspicion— particularly in light of the second leading aspect of experts, namely the intractable conflicts among them. In 1894, William Edward Quine remarked that "the status of expert testimony is the scandal and disgrace of the medical profession. The so-called expert is employed not because he is an expert physician, not because he is an expert diagnostician or an expert therapeutist, but because he is an expert swearer."[6] The fact that two well-certified individuals can offer oathbound testimonies in direct contradiction naturally creates public resistance. Gove's bombshell—people are tired of experts—caught the force of a still wider, and likely growing, suspicion of the rituals of intellectual authority. Someone is introduced—in court, on television, at the lectern—as "expert," and the assumption is that he/she is beyond lay critique. But the ready-to-hand exposure of conflict among authorities and their failure to reach agreement becomes an instrument of contempt, well honed in the media. The *Daily Telegraph* reported Gisela Stuart, another Leave campaigner, as saying that "There is only one expert that matters, and that's you, the voter," and cited a caller to Radio 2's Jeremy Vine, who noted that experts "built the Titanic."[7]

When the supporters of Remain (in the European Union) saw the danger of the challenge, they spoke out quickly. David Cameron, the soon to be resigning prime minister, insisted that "Credible experts [warn] about risks to our economic security" and that the opportunities "for your children and your grandchildren . . . depends on the strength of our economy and I believe—along with this collection of independent experts—that our economy is stronger inside this organization . . . So listen to the experts." In the event, of course, most didn't. The nation's leading economists prepared a letter making a version of Cameron's case, and part of the shock effect of the vote was the dawning recognition, especially among economists, that urgent appeals could be so casually ignored.

Part of Cameron's hurried harried response was to invoke a standard tactic in the arguments. You wouldn't build a bridge or a house "without expert advice."[8] Why then would you ignore the World Trade Organization or the chairman of the US Federal Reserve? The maneuver is familiar. An area of ambiguous judgment is mapped onto the hierarchy of engineering, mathematics, or rocket science. But a fair question is whether the analogy is right and the mapping legitimate. It lets us see that part of the difficulty—one that becomes pressing in the humanities—is with the word itself. "Expert" seems to travel smoothly across intellectual fields and departments of knowledge—but only seems.

The conceptual issue has become pointed in the last few years. Partly, this is due to the changing historical situation, epitomized by the Brexit campaign, where tensions between a knowledge elite and a resentful public become inescapable. But partly, too, it's a question of changing views within the institutions of academic life. The term is not only everywhere in the press; it informs the way academic knowledge understands itself; and it has become especially prominent in efforts to evaluate academic success. When the UK Research Excellence Framework (REF) announced the 2014 evaluation, the concept of expertise was foundational. It rings like a bell all through the prospectus, accompanied by the equally obsessive chanting of the nearby word "excellence." An opening passage notes that "The REF will be a process of expert review. Expert sub-panels for each of 36 units of assessment (UOAs) will carry out the assessment, working under the leadership and guidance of four main panels."[9] A few pages later comes the symphonic crescendo:

> The REF is a process of expert review. Recent consultations about reforms to the assessment framework confirmed widespread confidence in discipline-based expert review founded upon expert judgement. To maintain confidence in the assessment process and in the credibility of the outcomes to those being assessed, we have appointed panels of experts who are currently or have recently been active in high quality research, or its wider use. While these experts will draw on appropriate quantitative indicators to support their professional judgement, expert review remains paramount.[10]

Much of interest lies in these words, but for the moment, the sheer mere dependence on the word "expert" deserves some thought, as does the lazy assumption that we know what we mean when we use it.

In *Toward a General Theory of Expertise* (1991), Ericsson and Smith set out to carve precision from the ambiguity. In their careful words, the aim was "to understand and account for what distinguishes outstanding individuals in a domain from less outstanding individuals in that domain, as well as from people in general."[11] The problem becomes a question for empirical psychology: how to design experiments to capture the distinction between outstanding achievement and the rest. A requirement is comparison under "standardized conditions,"[12] within "domains in which there are accepted measures of performance"[13]— that is, domains where measurement is possible and precise. Professional chess is a favored example. It divides among masters, experts, and novices, and its system of ranking opens to quantitative reading. From the standpoint of the *General Theory*, analysis depends upon "exacting methodological criteria, particularly the criterion that superior performance should be demonstrated as well as captured by a collection of laboratory tasks."[14] You identify standard tasks that allow for outstanding performance; you create a set of replicable conditions, compare attainments, and correlate superior outcomes with certain cognitive processes (memory, attention, perception, discernment). Then you will have measured expertise.

The instruments may be precise, but their yield is meager. In the absence of repeatable, quantifiable performance, the theory has nothing to offer. "In some cases," the authors concede, "the lack of success in capturing the essence of an expertise is so well documented that there may not be a legitimate phenomenon to study."[15] Surely, though, the point is a narrowness in method, rather than an absence of experts. In common use, expertise appears throughout the social/cultural field: we have no reason to believe that many cases resemble the situation of chess. Indeed, the very constraints in the Ericsson–Smith approach generate the problem, which is exactly the various dimensions of expertise within different fields of action. The work of this chapter is to follow separate currents in the history of the puzzlement, currents that have largely run separately from one another. Bringing them together should help outline what's at stake in the controversies and how they bear on the fate of the humanities.

The Courtroom, Junk Science, and Science Studies

> "No one will deny that the law should in some way effectively use expert knowledge wherever it will aid in settling disputes. The only question is as to how it can do so best."[16]

Daubert v. Merrell Dow Pharmaceuticals Inc.,[17] the 1993 decision of the Supreme Court, set still prevailing terms for allowing expert testimony in the U.S. courtroom. The judgment overturned a 1923 ruling known as the "Frye standard," which had permitted expert evidence as long as it enjoyed "general acceptance in the particular field in which it belongs."[18] The ambiguity of the formulation had become notorious. But it wasn't until the end of the century that the court tried to clarify judicial theory and courtroom practice, with only slightly less notoriety.

The case, the decision, and its controversies raise issues well beyond the legal domain.

What makes the difficulties of expertise so pointed within the law is, of course, that momentous outcomes are at stake, while the questions are difficult. How should judge and jury avail themselves of special claims to knowledge? What relation does expert testimony hold toward the testimony of ordinary "fact" witnesses? On what ground can expertise be established?

The problems are long-standing. An early practice in English law, datable to the fifteenth century, had been to impanel a "special jury" of those with relevant practical knowledge. Learned Hand refers to a trial of 1645 in which a court convened a jury of merchants "because it was conceived they might have better Knowledge of the Matters in Difference which were to be tried, than others could, who were not of that Profession."[19] In another legal arrangement, also emphasized by Hand, a court would summon individuals suited to illuminate puzzling facts—doctors who could tell if a wound was fresh, or grammarians who could parse some opaque Latin. Only slowly did there emerge the pattern of expert witnesses brought forward by the contending parties: expert v. expert. Predictably, when authoritative speech is claimed on both sides of the question and two credentialed witness differ, the aura of authority wanes. Jennifer Mnookin cites a lawyer who noted (in 1899) that expertise "is the subject of everybody's sneer, and the object of everybody's derision. It has become a newspaper jest. The public has no confidence in expert testimony."[20]

Nearly a century later, the plaintiffs in *Daubert* argued for admitting testimony that indicated the drug Benedictin could cause birth defects. Even though scientists making the claim possessed eminent credentials and had relied on rigorous studies (animal and test-tube research, the reinterpretation of statistical conclusions), their work had not (yet) won consensus in the scientific community. They were therefore challenged on the basis of the Frye standard of "general acceptance." The Supreme Court weighed the competing claims—rigorous science vs. existing consensus—claims that were also clashing legal theories. The opinion, written by Judge Blackmun, held that the Frye standard had been superseded by the Federal Rules of Evidence of 1975, of which Rule 702 asserts that expert knowledge can be admitted if it "will assist the trier of fact" (judge or jury).

The key assumption is that expertise can be reliably ascertained, that it meets rigorous criteria, distinguishing legitimate from illegitimate evidence. Two years before *Daubert*, Peter W. Huber had published *Galileo's Revenge: Junk Science in the Courtroom*, a book raising the specter of specious testimony swamping the pursuit of scientifically informed legal judgment. The task for the Supreme Court was to find principles that would secure working distinctions and prevent the cynical use of mere seeming science, peddled by posing experts. The decision in *Daubert* placed heavy responsibility on the trial judge, who "must ensure that any and all scientific testimony or evidence admitted is not only relevant, but reliable." Crucially, the knowledge in question must be "derived by the scientific method."[21]

A bracing historical irony is that the *Daubert* decision coincided with the maturing of Science Studies as a newly influential program of academic research. The result was that efforts to settle the question of courtroom expertise developed alongside a powerful, often polemical revisionary theory. Notably, when Justice Blackmun characterizes scientific knowledge on the grounds of "testability," he recalls the mid-century orthodoxy derived from Karl Popper's philosophy of science. Reference is made to the famous/notorious concept of falsifiability, used to distinguish science from pseudoscience. On its basis, Popper had controversially dismissed Marxism and psychoanalysis: since no observation or experiment could refute these theories, they had no claim to the status of science. As Popper put it in the passage quoted in *Daubert*, "[T]he criterion of the scientific status of a theory is its falsifiability, or refutability, or testability."[22]

Much of the late twentieth-century impetus behind Science Studies came from a refusal of Popper's criterion. Thomas Kuhn's work, especially in *The Structure of Scientific Revolutions*, challenged the idea that even the most rigorous of sciences developed through observation–experiment–refutation. In practice, scientists held to existing theories even in the face of apparent failure; no methods of "testability" or "refutability" can offer definitive rejection, given both the intellectual flexibility of science and its complex institutional life. It's been especially the second emphasis upon the norms, habits, and embedded practices of institutions that became prominent in the work that followed Kuhn.

By the time the Supreme Court was establishing the rules of expert testimony on the basis of "scientific knowledge," work in Science Studies had already disputed central assumptions on which the decision was based. Three years after *Daubert*, Sheila Jasanoff offered some crisp unsettling words, noting that "the attempt to reassess in a legal forum what scientists know, and how they come to know it, threatens to put both judges' and attorneys' lay conceptions of 'the scientific method' on a collision course with scientists' actual practice."[23] Pointing to recent turns in the sociology and philosophy of science, the essay captures the instability of the mid 1990s, when developments within two different domains were moving in contrary directions.

Jasanoff, a leading figure in Science Studies, lays out propositions that had become broadly shared, all resting on the insight that even rigorous procedures could never eliminate impurity: there are "no abstract universally applicable standards against which the validity of scientific facts can be tested."[24] Here is the terse refusal of Popper's falsifiability. No universal standards, and no resting on ideals of shared observation. Too many cases reveal contradiction, even over questions of experimental replication, or over what constitutes an experiment or a finding. The assumption that "formal principles" underlie the determination of truth has too often been exposed as unfounded. In fact, there is "prior negotiation and consensus building," nothing as crystalline as incontestable truth, but an ongoing process of "tacit knowledge, experience and skill."[25] Even as the court depended on the clarity of scientific method, Science Studies was creating dense pictures of inevitably unclear procedures. Within its frame, the appeal to "testability" was a crudely simple reduction, likely to bring more, not less, confusion to the courtroom.

The sequence is worth preserving. Through the seventies and eighties came a series of major environmental and toxic tort claims;[26] in 1991, Huber's book on junk science appeared; in 1993, the *Daubert* decision was delivered; and soon afterwards came the rejoinders from Science Studies, of which Jasanoff's 1996 essay is an epitome. The anxiety about dubious, "junk" science, the legal attempt to fortify the standing of experts, and then the skeptical, sociological critique of any formal guarantees of expertise—the events of the early nineties made a clash of views unavoidable. When it came, the disputes led to an unsettling of confidence persisting over two decades. Much more recently, in 2013, a National Commission on Forensic Science was convened whose objective was precisely to strengthen "the validity and reliability"[27] of expert testimony in the criminal justice system. At the time of this writing, its report has not been published.

The history of Science Studies in the last two generations suggests that a critique of expertise is not simply a populist reaction but grows out of a systematic rethinking of expert knowledge. The reliability of science can be taken as neither transparent nor simple. The conflicts among experts lay bare the workings of other pressures and factors, partly intellectual but partly social/institutional. Furthermore, the issue sharpens when the clashing experts stand before a resistant public. For this last aspect, we turn to another event of late twentieth-century history and a different arena of contention.

After the 1986 disaster at Chernobyl, the British government restricted sheep farming in Wales and Cumbria, with the Food Standards Agency originally placing limits on nearly 10,000 farms. As long as sheep showed signs of radioactive cesium isotopes absorbed through grazing, they were immobilized and slaughtered. Only over time, and at great cost to the farmers, were the restrictions removed, with the last disappearing in 2012.

The explosion in Russia opened a new line of inquiry into the social standing of expert judgment. Two essays by Brian Wynne that address the Chernobyl aftermath stand alongside Jasanoff's work, challenging theoretical complacency through close case study.[28] Wynne's interviews with affected sheep farmers exposed "the Expert-Lay Knowledge Divide," which, as he shows, changed rapidly within the brief period after the disaster. Initially, the British public was assured there was no risk to farming or to the food chain. Six weeks later, the government suddenly put a ban on the slaughter and sale of the animals. Again, confident words suggested the suspension would be short-lived (no more than three weeks), but after a first month the restrictions were extended with no end in sight. Gradually the critical area narrowed to 150 farms, a vulnerable "crescent" that had another notable feature: namely its proximity to the Sellafield nuclear complex. Sellafield had long been the site of massive ongoing nuclear activity: processing, reprocessing, and storing. The plant gave work to thousands of employees; its history since the 1950s has been marked with controversy (including a disastrous

fire of 1957 that released radioactive iodine and cesium in the area).
In September of this year (2016), a *Panorama* documentary on BBC
television reported that the site "was riddled with potentially lethal
safety flaws."[29]

Wynne's recovery of the local history shows how sheep farmers
had lived alongside Sellafield with little obvious uneasiness or social
friction. But the confusions after Chernobyl stirred up mistrust that
had been buried within the community. As experts repeatedly failed to
explain why the radioactivity persisted, farmers revealed their own
suspicions: namely, that the real cause of the radioactivity was not
the recent release in Chernobyll but a decades-long poisoning from
Sellafield. The failure of expert knowledge in 1986—the guarantees
and their withdrawal, the changing explanations of the scientists, their
ignorance of the sheep grazing that they were now closely regulating—
undermined the old promises that Sellafield posed no threat to the
sheep. The farmers saw:

> that the scientists had made unqualified reassuring assertions,
> then been proven mistaken, and had not even admitted making
> a serious mistake. Their exaggerated sense of certainty and
> arrogance was a major factor in undermining the scientists'
> credibility with the farmers on other issues such as the source
> of the contamination. In any case the typical scientific idiom of
> certainty and control was culturally discordant with the farmers,
> whose whole cultural ethos routinely accepted uncertainty
> and the need for flexible adaptation rather than prediction and
> control.[30]

Part of the significance of Wynne's account is its attentiveness to popular
resistance to expert knowledge and its exposure of the unfounded certainty in the rhetoric of government/science utterance. The farmers
noted the inconsistencies of authoritative speech, and, in this aspect,
the episode takes its place within the broader corrosions of expert
"credibility." But the other thread in Wynne's accounts follows not the
critical, but the affirmative, knowledge-work of the farming community. As scientists and other officials trod the hills of Cumbria, they
applied the data to their models in the accepted manner, but in so
doing, they walked clumsily over the time-honored practices of hill
grazing. The farmers became observers with close-hand "experience

of watching scientists decide where and how to take samples, of seeing
the variability in readings over small distances, of noticing the difficulty of obtaining a consistent standard for background levels, and
of gradually becoming aware of the sheer number and variety of
less controlled assumptions and judgments that underpin scientific
facts."[31] The scientists, on the other hand, paid little mind to the styles
of knowledge by which the farmers work and live. Hill sheep farming,
notes Wynne, is "a highly specialist and particular kind of farming," but
it is an "expertise...not coded anywhere," passed on by apprenticeship
through a craft tradition.[32] In a statement that delivers a foundational
insight for Science Studies in the nineties, Wynne holds that "The
implicit moral imperative driving science is to recognize and control
the world so as to iron out contradiction and ambiguity."[33] Not only
does this imperative distort the uncontrolled, institutional/political
contexts of science, but it also overlooks the active world of everyday
knowledge, local expertise.

Dewey vs. Lippmann: What Can the Public Know?

Both the legal debates over the *Daubert* judgment and the rise of
Science Studies stand within a longer background that goes under the
misleading name of the Dewey–Lippmann debate. When Walter
Lippmann's *Public Opinion*[34] appeared in 1922, John Dewey reviewed it
in *The New Republic*;[35] and when Lippmann followed with a second
book, *The Phantom Public* (1925),[36] Dewey was again the reviewer.
No real exchange between the two constituted a "debate" or even
significant exchange of views. But the contrast between their positions
is evident, becoming conspicuous during that same period of the early
1990s, this time within the realm of communication and media studies.
It offers a useful third lineage.

At the core of Lippmann's position was a self-conscious even
flamboyant provocation. The modern world was too complicated
for a democratic public. The sophistication of science, the intricacy
of the economy, and the power of new technologies, far elude the
understanding of the ordinary citizen. Only experts in their fields
are qualified to make the decisive judgments on which the future of
modernity depends. The expert represents "the unseen. He represents
people who are not voters, functions of voters that are not evident,

events that are out of sight, mute people, unborn people, relations between things and people. He has a constituency of intangibles."[37] As Michael Schudson well emphasizes, Lippmann's experts make no policy decisions themselves, but rather advise policymakers with a pure disinterested detachment.[38] Their responsibility is to offer guiding knowledge through the formidable challenges of the postwar world; they alone will have the depth of experience and the precision of insight.

Dewey's first review begins by praising the brilliance of *Public Opinion*, which he finds so elegantly presented that the reader can finish the text without realizing that "it is perhaps the most effective indictment of democracy... ever penned." For Lippmann, writes Dewey, public opinion "is casual, the product of limited contact with the environment of facts and forces... shaped chiefly by tradition, by stereotyped pictures, and by emotions, by personal interests unintelligently conceived."[39] Seen thus, the threat lies in giving too great a role to an ill-equipped and easily misled public, when, in fact, the only way to sustain democratic government is to diminish the power of public opinion. Theories of democracy suppose that the voter is an "omnicompetent, sovereign citizen," but this is an "unattainable ideal."[40] No voting public can ever achieve the mastery required for decisive action; it has neither the training nor the skill nor the time. Citizens have the power to select their rulers, but that power only becomes significant in times of emergency ("a reserve of force brought into action during a crisis in public affairs"[41]). Even here, the role of the public is negative: "It does not reason, investigate, invent, persuade, bargain or settle. But by holding the aggressive party in check, it may liberate intelligence."[42] At bottom, the public does no more than secure the legitimacy of government. "To support the Ins when things are going well, to support the Outs when they seem to be going badly, this, in spite of all that has been said about Tweedledum and Tweedledee, is the essence of popular government."[43] Within a better and more stable arrangement, the public would accept this modest role; it would not pretend to the competence of policymaking; it would vote and then recede, leaving experts to generate the most important facts and most efficient theories, unencumbered.

Dewey's generous response is to grant the suave power of Lippmann's critique, to accept its coherence, and to agree that the figure of an "omnicompetent" citizen, adequate to the urgencies of action, is a sentimental delusion. But for Dewey, to accept the privilege of expertise—even under the demanding conditions of modernity—is to surrender hope in the democratic project. He admits confusion within the public sphere, but insists a democratic citizenry can attain the consciousness and self-consciousness fit for a political vocation. The way forward is not through the remote deliberations of experts but through an education of the public: "There can be no public without full publicity in respect to all the consequences which concern it. Whatever obstructs and restricts publicity, limits and distorts public opinion."[44] His argument is not that an already existing public can be a competent decision-maker, but that its right to the role must be defended and that the task of education is to prepare it for responsibilities it should never disown.

Here a striking but neglected emphasis in Lippmann raises the stakes of the contrast. As the book works out details of the age of expertise, *Public Opinion* proposes a new social role for those entrusted with knowledge. The power of the expert "depends upon separating himself from those who make the decisions, upon not caring in his expert self, what decision is made,"[45] because "the expert represents no strength available in the immediate."[46] Each department of government should have its own "permanent intelligence section"; each must be granted independence, ensured through "funds, tenure, and access to the facts."[47] Indeed, "Tenure should be for life, with provision for retirement on a liberal pension, with sabbatical years set aside for advanced study and training, and with dismissal only after a trial by professional colleagues."[48] If all this suggests an uncanny resemblance to the modern university, Lippmann is not slow to draw the conclusion. The intelligence bureaux of government would constitute a central agency, committed to the rigors of inquiry—"problems of definition, of terminology, of statistical technic, of logic"—without regard for policy or practical effect:

> The work need not all be done in Washington, but it could be done in reference to Washington. The central agency would, thus, have the makings of a national university. The staff could be recruited there for the bureaus from among college graduates. They would be working on theses selected after consultation

between the curators of the national university and teachers
scattered over the country. If the association was as flexible as it
ought to be, there would be as a supplement to the permanent
staff, a steady turnover of temporary and specialist appointments
from the universities, and exchange lecturers called out from
Washington.[49]

We take Dewey as the great modern philosopher of education, but we
should recognize Lippmann as a contending philosopher. Experts are
the preserving forces of modernity. Because they alone can organize the
knowledge through which governments manage a complex world, they
must be separated from practicality, protected from distorting pressure, and set free to pursue truth without care for consequences.
Yet the justification of independence is a higher practicality. The work
will always be done "in reference to Washington." By staying immune
from immediate demand, experts can best serve the making of policy,
which for Lippmann is the only point of expertise. This argument,
lightly sketched in both books, will become a dominant paradigm in
the defense of universities as homes of independent inquiry, relieved
from pressures of immediacy, but finally justified through the practical
effects of practice-neglecting inquiry.

Notice that within Lippmann's circuit of exchange, no place is
given to the public itself. The ordinary citizen will be ever unsuited to
the tasks of research and policy. Even for Dewey, the imperfection
must be granted. An omnicompetent public remains an ideal that can
only be realized, if ever, at the end of a long history. Until then, dis-
tortion will remain; it cannot be wished away. What comes quickly to
the surface in the Dewey/Lippmann contrast is the chasm between
expert and public, and the conviction (shared by both) that, in the
world we now inhabit, the average citizen must yield to those who
truly know.

The puzzles over *Wikipedia* return here. Recall Larry Sanger's dispute
with Jimmy Wales in the early stages of the project, Sanger insisting
there could be no "credible *encyclopedia* without oversight by experts"
and that *Wikipedia*'s "root problem" was "anti-elitism, or lack of respect
for expertise." From his point of view, as severely coherent as Lippmann's,
the public was more than a corruption; it was an interference.[50] Well
into the development of the encyclopedia and even in the face of

its success, Sanger was calling for "management by experts"[51] and regretting the power of the community to discourage participation, or at least the active presence, of expert voices. Woe to the expert who "should have the gall to complain to the community about the problem, he or she will be shouted down (at worst) or politely asked to 'work with' persons who have proven themselves to be unreasonable (at best)."[52]

Sanger frequently writes as if expertise were an attainment of inner character, which once achieved will always incarnate proper qualification. Ph.D in hand, the expert stands out as clearly distinct from the "community," which is so often intemperate and unreasonable. Why, he asks, would any proper academic risk the indignity of these encounters? He predicts that "nearly everyone with much expertise but little patience will avoid editing Wikipedia, because they will—at least if they are editing articles on articles that are subject to any sort of controversy—be forced to defend their edits on article discussion pages against attacks by nonexperts." He also assumes that this division will rend *Wikipedia* in two: "I do not see how there can *not* be a more academic fork of the project in the future."[53] If *Wikipedia* remains the encyclopedia that "anyone can edit,"[54] the expert version will set up boards of management and peer review.

Sanger's distinction is familiar and plausible. Indeed, in the years since his early challenges, attempts have been made to establish academic versions of the project. The struggle is one that *Nupedia* faced in the days before it went wiki: the university-based contributors have been painfully slow to submit or to review copy, which made any encyclopedic goal recede into the distance. But the more serious difficulty concerns the status and semantics of expertise itself. Sanger's faith in credentials, in the mere holding of a Ph.D, is touching. But against the background of law, science, and Lippmann–Dewey, what *Wikipedia* can suggest to theory is that the practice of the expert is more unsettled and more interesting than he assumes.

The issue returns us to the disputes within legal theory. The *Daubert* decision of 1993 depended on hard distinctions between the ordinary fact witness and expert testimony. Only the expert has the right to summarize observations, to offer opinions, and to draw conclusions. Yet, the body of theory in the last generation has shown how untenable this distinction has also become. The judge must stand at the gate, keeping out evidence that does not meet standards of rigorous and credentialed knowledge. But as we have seen, this demand on the court met a near-simultaneous turn in Science Studies, which threw caustic doubt on the clarity of such knowledge. *Daubert* was founded on a weakened conception of "scientific validity." In Larry Laudan's words, "The quest for a specifically scientific form of knowledge or for a demarcation criterion between science and non-sciences, has been an unqualified failure. There is apparently no epistemic feature or set of such features which all and only the 'sciences' exhibit."[55] Then, beyond the theoretical quandaries, it came to seem unreasonable to ask judges to decide what passed scientific muster, to take on the burden of making distinctions without possessing stable criteria.

Part of what lay behind *Daubert*, as Simon Cole has emphasized, was an anxiety about the dangerous power that an "expert" might wield, the fear that "some expert evidence has the potential to be particularly misleading and therefore poisonous to the fact-finder, so poisonous indeed that the fact-finder must be protected from the expert."[56] A result is the requirement that judges sift real science from junk science and do so by applying articulate criteria. "Junk" is invidious. It's easy enough to find egregious cases of false reasoning, but much harder to draw settled lines that will keep the clean and the dirty safely apart. Cole's formulation is telling: "The Court mandated a dichotomous framework for evaluating expert evidence. In the gatekeeping framework, evidence is either admissible or inadmissible. This is plainly inconsistent with the nature of expert evidence itself, which must be arrayed along a continuum of reliability."[57] In this view, there is no alternative to the "truth-producing engine" of cross-examination.[58] The dream of indubitable expertise is a judicial fallacy.

These terms of debate plainly intersect with other domains of expertise. What is it to claim such status? And what to be accorded it? When do we need it? And how far does it reach? Hilary Putnam has described a linguistic division of labor which distinguishes among the capacities of speakers to use certain words. Some speakers will know the full extension of a term. Others will use a word with only partial, though still correct, understanding. Others understand nothing of the meaning at all. Every linguistic community, suggests Putnam, "possesses at least some terms whose associated 'criteria' are known only to a subset of the speakers who acquire the terms, and whose use by the other speakers depends upon a structured cooperation between them and the speakers in the relevant subsets."[59] R. A. Sharpe draws on Putnam's work, expressing the distinction in more homely terms:

> Though I know what gold is and can generally apply the word correctly, in hard cases I defer to the expert. I cannot tell the difference between fool's gold and the genuine article, whilst a metallurgist can, so I naturally defer to him on the application of even such a widely used word as 'gold'. It is worth noting of just how many nouns this is true. I can use the word 'wryneck' up to a point; I know that it is a small bird whose head is characteristically turned to one side, but that is about the limit of my knowledge. I cannot tell the difference between a wryneck and a thrush.[60]

Here is another, and better, way of understanding Cole's proposal of a "continuum" rather than a "dichotomy." The lines of expertise run along many dimensions. One who quickly separates a wryneck from a thrush may fail to identify fool's gold. The division of expert labor is a network of crisscrossing skills and abilities with no common standard. The designation of chess mastery is numerically assigned, while expertise in skateboarding or joke-telling escapes both number and precision. Part of the difficulty comes back to the necessarily loose use of the term itself. "Expert" is everywhere. It still carries the semantic aura of credentialed accomplishment, but it also suggests a merely general tone of achievement. When Robert Burton nods to the greatness of Democritus in *The Anatomy of Melancholy*, he describes his precursor as "a great divine, according to the divinity of those times, an expert physician, a politician, an excellent mathematician," where "expert" is no more than one honorific in a series.[61] And when Michael Gove asserted that the British "have had enough of experts," his words rang loudly, in part because the term covered such a multitude of putative authorities: not only well-published economists but the many politicians, media presenters, academics, and officials who spoke in similar tones of authority.

A central aspect of the question concerns the boundaries of expertise, the limits of even well-tested mastery. The epigraph to this chapter gives Borges's reminder that "outside his own specialty," each is "credulous." So too, even within his ardent defense of a corps of government experts, Lippmann notes that "every one of us is an outsider to all but a few aspects of modern life",[62] much as Anthony Giddens remarks that "all specialists revert to being members of the ordinary lay public" as soon as they confront the "diverse arenas of expertise, that affect our lives today."[63] And beyond the figure of the expert who must also live as an ordinary citizen within an intricate world, there is the division of knowledge within the expert realms themselves, the exchange of privileged roles and institutional authority, of which the university is the most telling example.

Where Are Experts in the Humanities?

The university is not only a home, or a refuge, for the expert. It's also the place where expertise sees its limits, often many times a day. In the spirit of Borges's remark, Collins and Evans describe scientists, who "cannot speak with much authority at all outside their narrow field of specialization,"[64] and for reasons soon to be clearer, the limits are more visible in the humanities. In salient respects, the precision that establishes intellectual authority also draws its limits. In Giddens's trenchant words:

> The very specialization which expertise undergoes makes it obvious to everyone that there can be no 'experts of all experts' but that all expert claims to knowledge are not only very specific, but also liable often to be internally contested...The fact that experts frequently disagree becomes familiar terrain for almost everyone.[65]

Within the social geography of the university, the physical spread of departments is an image for the borders around knowledge. To enter another building, office, or laboratory is to transform from expert to novice. One's own proud accumulation of knowledge, not to mention one's record of publication, may dwindle quickly, even with apparently small changes of focus (a different period of history, a different language and culture).

For the humanities, issues of expertise are pervasive and elusive. We have some familiar-sounding cases with scholars who work for years on a well-bounded subject: a poem, a quartet, a painting, a prison, a proof. The goal is a scholarly encounter as exhaustive as possible, the object known in almost every crevice, turned toward every angle of light. Someone, you might say, has to do it. And yet, even when done proudly, it requires arduous commitment to keep command of just one career or just a single work. Even in these "narrow" cases there is exposure to changing perspectives or new challenge. Although it's less visible outside university settings, scholarship in the humanities knows that the most narrow inquiry is never comprehensive. It's always open to other ways of seeing that someone else has chosen to pursue. The history of the last hundred years is a record of multiplying axes of inquiry, and nothing is now more familiar than the endless articulation of research even within the closest quarters of specialization. A specialist in the biography of Mozart may be rank amateur in the history of his reception. A scholar of pigments in the Florentine Renaissance may know little about the elaborate networks of patronage.

As subfields in the humanities grow, especially with the enlargement of canons, then the distance between focused expertise and the borders of the discipline widens and lengthens. To those new to university-based research, it can be a surprise to find that the local logician has little to say to the epistemologist, or that the medievalist may not be concerned to read the latest by Martin Amis. It is, after all, a sensible surprise. At even a small distance away from the seminar room and the lecture hall, it seems fair to ask that an English professor should have read it all, at least once, or that the teacher of Beethoven should be able to discourse at length on American jazz. Nor is this only an outsider's naiveté. Many (most?) professing the humanities began in other periods or problems, began too with the determination to span the field, and continue to read "outside of period" and "to keep up with new novels."

From the perspective of everyday listeners, viewers, readers, the very point of professing a field is to traverse its breadth; to know the variety of styles, forms, and periods; not to enjoy all equally, but to inspect the plenitude. Some such attitude explains the satire directed at the figure of the desiccated specialist. It appears within the professoriate too, the half-disguised disdain, mixed with grudging respect, for the complete adept, the scholar untempted by other centuries or *oeuvres*. If critique takes on sharper edge in the contemporary humanities, this is largely because of institutional demands for broader competence: the need to examine, to teach, or to mentor across periods and problems. It remains a pointed and controversial question: how far the responsibility, and capability, of a professor should reach. Should training and experience prepare each faculty member to range the length of the discipline, if not to publish out of area; to make confident judgments on students and peers working on distant subjects and with different methods, to serve on examining or hiring committees for areas on which one has never taught or written or pontificated?

The term "expert" is only erratically applied, and not very usefully, in the humanities. It attaches most comfortably to those with competence in special methods, such as the handling of material objects, the identification of provenance, or the editing of musical scores or literary texts. It's a fair surmise that most scholars shy from the name of expert. Partly, this is due to rituals of humility. More significantly, it comes from recognition that most subjects, even the narrowest, attract a small crowd of others who share the focal object but who fathom aspects of it that one does not.

Careers grow too. For several generations now, the norm has not been the narrowly focused specialist but the multispecialist. A monograph under one thematic heading gives way to another, and you find a strong tendency for scholars to aim toward more general, sometimes more speculative work. The distinguished achievement of the historian Linda Colley gives one exemplary instance. A career that began with a book on the Tory Party 1714–1760 and a short book on Namier opened toward the capaciousness of *Britons: Forging the Nation:* 1707–1837 and the comparably large *Captives: Britain, Empire and the World,* 1600–1850. Most careers don't extend so widely or indeed so impressively. But they tend to avoid following the same line.

It can be more than a question of novelty. The demand for "an original contribution to knowledge" is a pillar, but it's fair to say that in the last half century, the humanities have inclined, not only to new thought, but even more, to the power of surprise. It's a distinct achievement to produce a thematic catalogue of Schubert's complete works or a concordance to the *Critique of Pure Reason.* Such work wins the praise it deserves. But higher acknowledgment has gone to works that overturn received wisdom or that offer audacious new syntheses. The force of books as different as J. L. Austin's *How to do Things with Words,* Sandra Gilbert and Susan Gubar's *The Madwoman in the Attic,* or E. H. Gombrich's *Art and Illusion,* resides partly in astonishment at the performance. The remarkable success of "theory" in the last half of the twentieth century came not only from the strength of insight, but from the examples of paradigm-shifting radicalism, the bravura acts of intellectual will. That it can be done at all, that foundational concepts and their relations can be redrawn—this has become an accepted and largely admiring recognition within the contemporary humanities. It has also become a practice imitated on a more modest scale, where it's been less accepted and admired. Even for those working in quieter registers or at younger stages in a career, the example of field-changing contributions is never far away. It can cast bright inspiring light, or it can be an ignis fatuus.

What makes it possible, sometimes pervasive, this bid for field-clearing astonishment? Much of an answer lies surely in the place of interpretation within the humanities. Not in every aspect, but in their leading and often defining terms, the humanities are interpretative and argumentative disciplines. Of course, this work appears in history quite differently from literature, and less markedly in bibliography than in art history. But the pattern of fixing on an object (event, text, problem, artifact); of directing attention to an array of details and contexts; and of proposing novel ways to relate these elements in order to open the object to new thought—this has been a dominant practice during the century of professionalization in the humanities. It need not have been so. It might have continued to favor recovery over interpretation, and presentation over argument. A monument such as Burckhardt's *The Civilization of the Renaissance in Italy* contains many presuppositions and syntheses; it never hesitates to propose meanings; it reflects deep-grained assumptions; and still it remains more committed to the display of what it has recovered than to new ways of seeing or understanding. Such an attitude persists. It raises a proud head, often in departments of history, whenever "concepts" seems to have fully devoured "facts." And yet the prominence of interpretation has been inescapable.

A science-in-humanities—to say it again—must remain part of our self-understanding. The empirical work of securing details of text, object, and event, including their material and technical conditions: this labor is close cousin to the precisionism in the laboratory. It cannot be forgotten. But the science-in-humanities is secondary, even when it's originary. Few scholars know how to handle the applications of patina, just as few converse easily about watermarks in the paper used by Alexander Pope. These few, as I've said, can wear the name "expert" without embarrassment. If this indispensable work remains secondary, it's only because the history of the humanities runs more centrally toward interpretation achieved through argument. Here, of course, is where the work is most vulnerable to critique and self-critique.

Interpretation has had its own desire for science and authority, for a strongly consensual set of norms and practices. The great systems of reading—including Christian hermeneutics, Marxism, psychoanalysis, structuralism—aimed toward a systematic apparatus of explanation. Differences of view were to be overcome; the conflict of interpretation would give way to canonical explanation. However, to write from the vantage point of the present (no one having come up with an alternative) is to recognize that we dwell at a moment of ineliminable pluralism. Humanists, to resume an earlier thought, are more likely to speak of their "lens" than their "theory"—in acknowledgment that other lenses would produce different foci. In most fields, to engage the act of interpretation is to grant, sometimes explicitly, always implicitly, that other perspectives are not only available, but equally credible. Academic publishers enjoy producing handbooks and casebooks, where essays on the same text or problem can be approached from several perspectives (e.g. feminist, psychoanalytic, new historicist). We now have ample resources (lenses) for the invention of interpretive novelties without end, and for some, this fact suggests a decadence and a pointlessness. Anyone who lives in a classroom or reads an academic journal will encounter strong new readings alongside implausible proposals that leap from evidence to hypothesis with abandon.

Yes, it can be tiresome, but it's the defect of a virtue. The willingness to test a risky hypothesis and to see the parts of a canvas, a score, or a text as having a structure never before recognized—this act can be performed crudely and embarrassingly. Still, it's the blood flow. In a lecture hall at University College London in the 1980s, Richard Wollheim reflected on the charge that Freud's interpretations constantly outstripped his evidence. Wollheim's response was that interpretation is as primary as evidence, and that although it can be offered rashly, unpersuasively, incoherently, the interpretive act cannot always wait for all evidence. It must make do with what it has. The dangers are evident, but so are the dangers of cautious refusal to build theory, even speculative theory.

The result is noise and impatience, but also the excitement of testing ambition, the attempt to secure larger understanding, always in the knowledge that some strong claim will have to be adjusted or retracted, and some oversight corrected. Evidence, and also rival interpretation, inevitably wear down the supremacy of the most brilliant thought. The period since World World II saw the immense reach in the work of, say, E.P. Thompson, Simone de Beauvoir, Ludwig Wittgenstein. Their after-histories brought challenge and amendment, small and large, but can anyone believe their thought should have been more modest? Or that we cease to move in its illumination, even after we reject basic principles and assumptions? That their (re)interpretations should have been less extreme?

But are they *experts*, even the large ones, the Wittgenstein, the de Beauvoir? The singularity of interpretation, the novelty, the astonishment make the biggest works not easily comparable to anything else. Expert relative to what? Within the humanities, the award of a prize is more widely understood than the claim to be expert, the prize typically in acknowledgment for distinctiveness of achievement that needn't imply a special place in a system of ranking. Indeed, the humanities are well suited to free us from the mystique of expertise. The word shares an etymology with "experience," and I note Collins and Evans's argument that "If there is to be a general criterion of expertise, experience is the leading candidate."[66] But we can go further and see "experience" not only as criterion for expertise, but as itself the better term, because it puts the emphasis where it belongs, not on a kind of person, but on a record of work and achievement. We then avoid granting a mysterious aura to the expert, the special power that Sanger seems to locate in the granting of a Ph.D. A proven familiarity with many dimensions of a problem, a history of contribution to the inquiry, the respect of others working in the field—these are the broadly reliable signs we want. But they should not be taken as marks of permanent endowment. No one can claim authority simply by framing a diploma on the wall. It's a weakness, both of academic credentializing and journalist credulity, that once an expert, always an expert—or very nearly so. In fact, of course, knowledge changes quickly, the young arrive without cease, and authoritative work of a decade past can seem quaint. Naturally, some thinkers preserve and enhance the work that warrants their high standing. But many more turn to other subjects and problems, relinquishing the old concerns, reluctant themselves to claim authoritative judgment. Experience that counts must change as fields of knowledge evolve. Finally, to speak of "experience" rather than "the expert" is to recognize that any complex question will require not one magus, but the plural insights of several (or many) contributors.

Knowledge by the Bootstraps: The "Un-Disciplined"

It's unlikely that those who sponsor the Research Excellence Framework will soon be replacing "expert" with "experienced," but it would better represent the practice of knowledge in the university, and beyond. Beyond, too, is where other signs of experience can be found. When Zhao and Bishop asked contributors to *Wikipedia* to identify the motivations behind their unpaid work, a significant number responded that it was a chance "to feel like experts."[67] The phrase can give useful pause: what can it mean to *feel like* an expert? Something wistful haunts the remark, the desire for the status, or glamour, of high intellectual status. But there's also something of hope and confidence, a belief that it's possible to command a body of knowledge wherever one is situated.

Almost anyone who works in academic zones has a memory of being approached by an enthusiast who asks for a minute. Maybe it's an oblique eccentric passion: syphilis in the bloodstream as predicting Marlow's course up the Congo River in *Heart of Darkness*, or a new Vermeer, or the real reason Beethoven withdrew the dedication of the "Eroica" to Napoleon. It's never graceful. Your face goes bland; you summon patience; you beg your phone to ring. You don't feel quite right about any of it. Yet this is the easy case.

Less easy is when a different stranger approaches, also raising a subject with an urgency that roils the usual rhythms of conversation. But this time the interlocutor intersects with subjects of your own, shows deep knowledge that can only come from patient study. You may feel the uneasiness of not having returned recently to the text or score or painting or politician. Then it becomes clear that your guest knows something you don't know, or have never known, but probably ought to have done; that you don't have a good or quick reply; and that, yes, there might be something to learn here.

"Independent scholar" is a name coolly bestowed on those who win due respect despite lacking credential or institution. The humanities (in some fields more than others, in history more than most) have seen notable contributions from that community, which has become increasingly organized. The National Coalition of Independent Scholars has given prominence to the work of its members, advocating strenuously for indispensable research privileges:

> The issues of greatest concern to the Coalition have been access to libraries and journals, the policies of agencies that offer academic grants, and technology. Repeated investigations and surveys have found that most independent scholars succeed in patching together sufficient access to library services, but that they often have to surmount obstacles in order to do so.[68]

It's worth noticing, though, that, even in its ringing defense of independence, the NCIS accepts the need for professional norms and necessities. Although its membership is identified as those who work outside academic institutions, it has its own requirements: "Membership is open to independent scholars from all disciplines. Applicants are required to submit a CV demonstrating a record of scholarly publications and/or conference presentations. NCIS does not require advanced degrees, but it does expect applicants to show that they are actively carrying out work of scholarly merit."[69] Here again is the magnet of canonical forms of expertise, with its usual markers: publications, conferencing, etc.

There is another independence, however, one that does not organize in societies, pay membership dues, or meet the usual norms of achievement. Knowledge, real knowledge, can grow in any attic. It can live in an unbarbered head that has never published or presented and that knows nothing of the National Coalition of Independent Scholars. The discomfort that academic life has taught itself to parry—the claim of the uncredentialed, untrained, un-disciplined inquirer—should become uncomfortable again. A great failure of university-based professionals is to have narrowed the field of research to our own kind. Too many wrinkled noses have missed sniffing out new knowledge. It's not, after all, that we have filled in all the gaps that dot our academic fields. The ideal of "coverage" within a department— with all the relevant periods, problems, and authors treated by someone in some semester—is a hollow dream. No department can cover it all, or even come respectably close. Part of the unsettlement of *Wikipedia*, I've been wanting to say, lies in its perpetual opening of lines of inquiry that had not even been named as such before. Nor does it require *Wikipedia* to persuade anyone that emerging fields grow more quickly than budgets and that busy individual lives will always leave promising plots untilled. It's never really a surprise, and it should usually be an occasion for gratitude, to find that some have taken on ambitious projects of their own, unconstrained by grants or colleagues or protocols. We should learn new styles of greeting, warmer hand-shakes, and forms of affirmation and exchange.

Consider that a discipline knows itself by its subject matter, but extends credentials only to those who learn its methods. "Method" here includes all, but not only, rigorous procedures, instruments, and standards of evidence and argument. It also comprises tone of voice, body language, a fair dose of irony and self-irony, and general campus-nurtured savvy. This is not to say there are fixed recipes, either for publication or public bearing. But it's clear that many curious and committed questers fall outside even the flexible boundaries of acceptable, assimilable comportment. If the methods aren't followed, methods in both these narrow and wide senses of methodical, then even passionate interest in a subject will seem off-point or excessive. It's an achievement of professionalization whose costs must be counted alongside its benefits that subjects inspire interest, but only methods qualify insight to count within the ranks of research.

If the university were less walled garden and more open, permeable, discontinuous space, then not only would more knowledge be exchanged and refined, but the practice of knowledge-seeking would lose some unnecessary mystery and exclusion. The language of "expert" is all right. But it will be most useful if more carefully handled, and best of all if it conveys these connotations of "experienced," rather than "endowed with specialized insight and perched on a summit." They can, and do, change quickly, those in command of narrowly focused areas. It's well to accept that they can be complemented, and even exceeded, by those who have swotted it up on their own. For most who don't live in the neighborhood of academic language, the very word "discipline" keeps its ordinary connotations of limit and restraint.

Although they may be indifferent to method, the "un-disciplined" can contribute to inquiry, even without wearing the latest lens.

Not everyone will accept an invitation to know, or to become, the un-disciplined, but I offer it all the same. Of course, there are and will remain many advantages to remaining within the field one knows by training and tradition. But it cannot be denied that brilliantly exhilarating work has transgressed guiltlessly against boundaries and precedents. This is easy to see within great achievement that has reverberated across the humanities, work, say, by Bakhtin, Benjamin, and Butler. But it's also often true of less ambitious research that disregards the usual procedures (and tones) of its own or any discipline, and achieves force by availing itself of different perspectives on new objects. T. S. Eliot's remark that "there is no method except to be very intelligent" is trenchant and timely.[70] Disciplines should and will survive, as should the call to interdisciplinarity, but the place of the un-disciplined has been neglected for too long. If the word suggests unruly and unrepentant attitudes, this can only to be to the good in settings where thought risks hardening.

Notes

1. Jorge Luis Borges, "The Secret Miracle" in *Ficciones* (New York: Grove Press, 1962), 144.
2. *Daily Telegraph*, June 10, 2016, http://www.telegraph.co.uk/news/2016/06/10/michael-goves-guide-to-britains-greatest-enemy-the-experts/, accessed May 17, 2017.
3. *Independent*, http://www.independent.co.uk/news/uk/politics/brexit-latest-news-michael-gove-nhs-claim-350m-twitter-vote-leave-eu-uk-a7498651.html, accessed May 17, 2017.
4. Martin Wolf, *Financial Times*, Jan 14, 2015.
5. Brian Wynne, "May the Sheep Safely Graze? A Reflexive View of the Expert–Lay Knowledge Divide," in Scott Lash, Bronislaw Szerszynski, and Brian Wynne, eds., *Risk, Environment and Modernity: Towards a New Ecology* (London: Sage, 1996), 48.
6. William Edward Quine, "Transactions of the Illinois State Medical Society," in Edward J. Huth and T. Jock Murray, eds., *Medicine in Quotations*, 2nd edn (Philadelphia, PA: American College of Physicians, 2006), 249.
7. http://www.telegraph.co.uk/news/2016/06/10/michael-goves-guide-to-britains-greatest-enemy-the-experts/, accessed May 17, 2017.
8. http://www.independent.co.uk/news/uk/politics/eu-referendum-david-cameron-boris-johnson-michael-gove-vote-leave-brexit-total-untruths-a7068871.html, accessed May 17, 2017.
9. http://www.ref.ac.uk/media/ref/content/pub/assessmentframeworkandguidanceonsubmissions/02_11.pdf, 1, accessed October 10, 2016.

10. Ibid., 4.
11. K. Anders Ericsson and Jacqui Smith, *Toward a General Theory of Expertise: Prospects and Limits* (Cambridge: Cambridge University Press, 1991), 2.
12. Ibid., 8.
13. Ibid., 9.
14. Ibid., 33.
15. Ibid., 33.
16. Learned Hand, "Historical and Practical Considerations Regarding Expert Testimony," *Harvard Law Review*, 15, 1 (May, 1901): 40.
17. Daubert v. Merrell Dow Pharmaceuticals Inc. 509 U.S. 579 (1993).
18. http://www.law.harvard.edu/publications/evidenceiii/cases/frye.htm, accessed May 17, 2017.
19. Hand, "Historical and Practical Considerations," 40.
20. Jennifer L. Mnookin, "Idealizing Science and Demonizing Experts: An Intellectual History of Expert Evidence," *Villanova Law Review*, 52, 763 (2007): 771.
21. http://caselaw.findlaw.com/us-supreme-court/509/579.html, accessed June 4, 2017.
22. Ibid.
23. Sheila Jasanoff, "Research Subpoenas and the Sociology of Knowledge," *Law and Contemporary Problems*, 59, 3 (Summer, 1996): 96.
24. Ibid., 98.
25. Ibid., 99.
26. Ibid., 95.
27. Ibid., 97.
28. Brian Wynne, "Misunderstood Misunderstanding: Social Identities and Public Uptake of Science," *Public Understanding of Science*, 1, 3 (1992): 281–304; "May the Sheep Safely Graze? A Reflexive View of the Expert–Lay Knowledge Divide," in Scott Lash, Bronislaw Szerszynski, and Brian Wynne, eds., *Risk, Environment and Modernity: Towards a New Ecology* (London: Sage, 1996): 44–83.
29. https://www.theguardian.com/environment/2016/sep/05/sellafield-nuclear-plant-riddled-safety-flaws-according-bbc-panorama#img-1, accessed May 17, 2017.
30. Wynne, "Misunderstood Misunderstanding": 287.
31. Ibid., 393.
32. Ibid., 295.
33. Ibid., 299.
34. Walter Lippmann, *Public Opinion* (New York: Macmillan Company, 1941).
35. John Dewey, Review of *Public Opinion, The New Republic*, May 3, 1922, 286–8.
36. Walter Lippmann, *The Phantom Public* (New York: Harcourt, Brace and Company, 1925).
37. Lippmann, *Public Opinion*, 382.
38. Michael Schudson, "The 'Lippmann–Dewey Debate' and the Invention of Walter Lippmann as an Anti-Democrat 1986–1996," *International Journal of Communication* 2 (2008), 1031–42.
39. Dewey, Review of *Public Opinion*, 286.
40. Lippmann, *The Phantom Public*, 39.
41. Ibid., 69.
42. Ibid., 69.

43. Ibid., 126–7.
44. John Dewey, *The Later Works of John Dewey*, 1925–1953, ed. J. A. Boydston (Carbondale, IL: Southern Illinois Press, 1969–90), vol. 2, 339.
45. Lippmann, *Public Opinion*, 382.
46. Ibid., 383.
47. Ibid., 386.
48. Ibid., 387.
49. Ibid., 392–3.
50. https://features.slashdot.org/story/05/04/18/164213/the-early-history-of-nupedia-and-wikipedia-a-memoir, accessed May 17, 2017.
51. Ibid.
52. http://larrysanger.org/2004/12/why-wikipedia-must-jettison-its-anti-elitism/, accessed May 17, 2017.
53. Ibid.
54. https://en.wikipedia.org/wiki/Main_Page, accessed May 17, 2017.
55. In Gary Edmond, "*Supersizing Daubert: Science for Litigation* and Its Implications for Legal Practice and Scientific Research," *Villanova Law Review*, 52, 763 (2007), 900.
56. Simon A. Cole, "Where the Rubber Meets the Road: Thinking about Expert Evidence as Expert Testimony," *Villanova Law Review*, 52, 763 (2007): 805.
57. Ibid.
58. Ibid.
59. Hilary Putnam, "The Meaning of 'Meaning,'" in *Mind, Language and Reality*, Philosophical Papers, vol. 2 (Cambridge: Cambridge University Press, 1975), 228.
60. R. A. Sharpe, "Art and Expertise," *Proceedings of the Aristotelian Society*, 85 (1984–5): 136.
61. Robert Burton, *The Anatomy of Melancholy* (New York: New York Review of Books, 2001), 16.
62. Lippmann, *Public Opinion*, 400.
63. Anthony Giddens, "Living in a Post-Traditional Society," in Ulrich Beck, Anthony Giddens, and Scott Lash, eds., *Reflexive Modernization: Politics, Tradition and Aesthetics in the Modern Social Order* (Stanford, CA: Stanford University Press, 1994), 89.
64. Harry Collins and Robert Evans, *Rethinking Expertise* (Chicago: University of Chicago Press, 2007), 145.
65. Giddens, "Living in a Post-Traditional Society," 186.
66. Collins and Evans, *Rethinking Expertise*, 53.
67. Xiaoli Zhao and M. J. Bishop, "Understanding and Supporting Online Communities of Practice: Lessons Learned from Wikipedia," *Educational Technology Research and Development*, 59, 5 (October 2011): 719.
68. http://www.ncis.org/interest, accessed May 17, 2017.
69. http://www.ncis.org/ncis-history, accessed May 17, 2017.
70. T. S. Eliot, *The Sacred Wood: Essays on Poetry and Criticism* (New York: Alfred A. Knopf, 1921), 10.

4

The Humanities in Time

Near the end of a century's pursuit of classical texts and the recovery of antiquity, the bookseller Vespasiano da Bisticci published a long series of short biographies. Among them was that of Poggio Bracciolini, scribe and manuscript quester, and more recently, protagonist in Stephen Greenblatt's *The Swerve: How the World Became Modern*.[1] For Greenblatt, the decisive event was Poggio's discovery of Lucretius' great work, *De Rerum Natura*, seen as the exemplary act in a world-historical transformation. Here is how Vespasiano presented Poggio at the great meeting in Constance, when, as the Catholic Church attempted to end the papal schism, he pounced.

> When the Council of Constance was assembled, Poggio went thither, and was besought by Nicolao and other learned men not to spare himself trouble in searching through the religious houses in these parts for some of the many Latin books which had been lost. He found six Orations of Cicero, and, as I understood him to say, found them in a heap of waste paper amongst the rubbish. He found the complete works of Quintillian [*sic*], which had hitherto been only known in fragments, and as he could not obtain the volume he spent thirty-two days copying it with his own hand: this I saw in the fairest manuscript. Every day he filled a copybook with the text. He found Tully's De Oratore, which had been long lost and was known only in parts ... and the poem of Lucretius, De rerum Natura.[2]

The other legendary pursuer of texts, appearing with Poggio in that first sentence, was Niccolò de' Niccoli, of whom Vespasiano writes:

> If he knew of any Greek or Latin book which was not in Florence he spared neither trouble nor cost until he should procure it ...

When it happened that he could only get the copy of a book he
would copy it himself, either in current or shaped characters, all
in the finest script, as may be seen in San Marco, where there
are many books from his hand in one lettering or the other.[3]

Niccoli also plays a leading part in Greenblatt's book, as Poggio's
friend and patron, sponsor of the classical recovery and a scribe in its
service. Unneeded in the narrative of *The Swerve*, Vespasiano himself
has no role. But in the different story at the beginning of this chapter,
the biographer has pride of place. There, at the end of the fifteenth
century, he memorialized his precursors who found the manuscripts
he now published and sold. In Florence, and then elsewhere, the
books had become intrinsic objects of value, marks of social and intellectual status, commodities for exchange, and the specification of a
life calling. For scholars, poet scholars, booksellers, and princes, for
a wider and growing community, and for a flourishing university, the
ancient texts oriented the practices of everyday life.

But the trove of information in the hundreds of sketches is not only
endless stimulus to scholars; it also marks a founding moment of
modern self-consciousness in the humanities. Vespasiano has no
pretensions as historian. But the accumulating effect of detail, data,
and anecdote is to create a sense of *period*—the fifteenth century as the
crystallization of efforts to make historical change, and to do so by
understanding one epoch against another. Questions of break and
continuity, of decline or improvement, of the coherence of culture,
these all move through Vespasiano's garrulous text.

Inheritance, Authority, Humility, Resistance

Without inheritance and transmission, no humanities. The humanities
live and compose themselves through time: each new practitioner has
predecessors and will have successors; vocation finds its meaning only
within a circuit of generations. Something is bequeathed, something
received, or rejected. The distance between generations may shrink,
even to a matter of months; the successor is sometimes older than the
predecessor; but response to the echo of earlier voices is inescapable
and inciting. Think, for instance, of the echo of Vespasiano's text. It lay
half-lost for hundreds of years, until Jacob Burckhardt encountered it

in the middle of the nineteenth century. As he embarked on his field-defining study of *The Civilization of the Renaissance in Italy*, Burckhardt acknowledged Vespasiano as the prod and stimulus, and also as one who measures the melancholy distance of the past:

> For further information as to the learned citizens of Florence at this period the reader must all the more be referred to Vespasiano, who knew them all personally, because the tone and atmosphere in which he writes, and the terms and condi- tions on which he mixed in their society, are of even more importance than the facts which he records.[4]

The relationship of Burckhardt to Vespasiano can be taken as a parable of the historical situation of the humanities. Burckhardt looks back to Vespasiano, who had looked at Federigo, Duke of Urbino, looking back:

> He alone had a mind to do what no one had done for a thousand years or more; that is, to create the finest library since ancient times. He spared neither cost nor labour, and when he knew of a fine book, whether in Italy or not, he would send for it.[5]

Federigo began with Latin poets and then:

> sought also all the known works on history in Latin, and not only those, but likewise the histories of Greek writers done into Latin, and the orators as well. The Duke also desired to have every work on moral and natural philosophy in Latin, or in Latin translations from Greek.[6]

As the ancient texts were to the Duke of Urbino, so the Duke was to Vespasiano, and Vespasiano to Burckhardt. When Stephen Greenblatt summons the booksellers of Florence, he makes the most recent link in this chain of descent. Such scenes exhibit the *generationalism* that constitutes the humanities. There are the texts that must be preserved, read, catalogued, interpreted, and taught. Then there are the gener- ations of scholars, who give way to later generations. A sense of short and long duration shows itself throughout Vespasiano's text: not only the debt to the past (past texts, past thinkers), but also the pressing awareness of the present tense within the motions of time. European philosophy may not consist in a "series of footnotes to Plato,"[7] but there is no escaping the generational reach that surrounds and shadows each task of thought. Even projects with no historical interest or dimension must negotiate with predecessors, most strenuously when earlier views are to be refused. Through almost every act in the humanities, the fields of study are no more important than the consciousness of precedent.

Inheritance is complex, fraught. Burckhardt's *Renaissance* plays out a central rhythm of reverence and critique. In his telling, the fifteenth-century Italians not only adored the Latin (and Greek) past, but aimed to restore it, to live it through again. Taking on its festivals and rituals, its language and literary forms, its names for children and claims of glory, they reached beyond continuity to identity. The past, without ceasing to be past, gave the form of the present. But such reverence wasn't an acquisition so much as an activity: ongoing, ever unfinished. It required the labor of the humanist scholars as well the generosity of patrons. These bore the standard of knowledge and the weight of value. To identify, appraise, compare, certify, interpret, reinterpret—such work is alive these six centuries later.

So too are its conflicts. In Burckhardt's unfolding narrative, the once-distinguished humanists discover that their vocation also lives in changing times. The authority of scholarship is never not vulnerable. The sense of a common project—discovery, preservation, interpretation—can be challenged at its foundations. It can indeed be most trenchantly challenged from within, as we read in these prophetic words:

> The first to make these charges were certainly the humanists themselves. Of all men who ever formed a class, they had the least sense of their common interests, and least respected what there was of this sense. All means were held lawful, if one of them saw a chance of supplanting another. From literary discussion they passed with astonishing suddenness to the fiercest and the most groundless vituperation. Not satisfied with refuting, they sought to annihilate an opponent.[8]

Faction within meets contempt without. By the middle of the sixteenth century, "The humanists, driven in other spheres from their commanding position, and viewed askance by the men of the Counter-reformation, lost the control of the academies: and here, as elsewhere, Latin poetry was replaced by Italian."[9] The fable of upheaval has been repeated many times since. In these days of ours, many of the old charges—"anger, vanity, obstinacy, self-adoration, a sinister influence on government, pedantry of speech, thanklessness towards teachers"[10]— are searingly familiar.

What makes Burckhardt a useful mirror is that his account gives rich terms for the generational predicament of the academic humanities and that he recognizes it as his own. His book offers both the aura of an authoritative work and the frank concession of partiality, as in the opening paragraph of *The Civilization of the Renaissance*:

> No one is more conscious than the writer with what limited means and strength he has addressed himself to a task so arduous. And even if he could look with greater confidence upon his own researches, he would hardly thereby feel more assured of the approval of competent judges. To each eye, perhaps, the outlines of a given civilization present a different picture; and in treating of a civilization which is the mother of our own, and whose influence is still at work among us, it is unavoidable that individual judgement and feeling should tell every moment both on the writer and on the reader. In the wide ocean upon which we venture, the possible ways and directions are many; and the same studies which have served for this work might easily, in other hands, not only receive a wholly different treatment and application, but lead also to essentially different conclusions.[11]

To locate perspectival thought in time is to acknowledge its fated limits. No one can read or remember enough. The individual character of so much research in the humanities inevitably raises questions of finite understanding, finite knowledge, stamina, will, years. Each wants to improve on what the past has given. Each prepares to become that past.

Samuel Johnson, at another founding moment, met this question. Editing Shakespeare, writing the poets' lives, compiling a dictionary— these determined individual acts were tangled in a web of precedent. He dismisses the myth of self-sufficiency, scorning Thomas Hamner for an edition that never acknowledged its dependence on the work of others. Yet Johnson knew that while depending on the "fortuitous discoveries of many men in devious walks of literature,"[12] he was also their adversary. Hoping to attain "superiority to his predecessors," he admits to having "the advantage of their labours."[13] The positive work of humane knowledge moves in cycles of destruction:

> Whoever considers the revolutions in learning...must lament the unsuccessfulness of enquiry, and the slow advances of truth, when he reflects, that great part of the labour of every writer is only the destruction of those that went before him. The first care of the builder of a new system, is to demolish the fabricks which are standing. The chief desire of him that comments an author, is to shew how much other commentators have corrupted and obscured him. The opinions prevalent in one age, as truths above the reach of controversy, are confuted and rejected in another, and rise again to reception in remoter times. Thus the human mind is kept in motion without progress.[14]

Johnson writes as a strong voice contending with other strength. Grand rivalry lives in our millennium too. But under the changing conditions of academic professionalism, the passage of generations takes on different aspects.

By the middle of the twentieth century, many disciplines in the humanities had defined themselves. They had also laid out terms of succession. On its face, the story is often a cheerful alternative to Johnson's "motion without progress." So the author of a recent study of genealogy places himself in a lineage of smooth descent, which he identifies as a common trope of academic self-understanding:

> [W]e seem to envision quasi-filial ties between doctoral students and their dissertation advisors, and use unmistakable genealogical diagrams to portray the flow of intellectual influence from Charles Peirce to John Dewey, Benedetto Croce to Antonio Gramsci, and Jeremy Bentham to John Stuart Mill. As I envision the quasi-intergenerational chain of mentors (Robert Park, Everett Hughes, and Erving Goffman) effectively connecting me to Georg Simmel, one of the 'founding fathers' of sociology, I therefore consider myself his 'great-great-grandstudent'.[15]

The picture has charm. But a fuller story requires less charm, fewer fathers, more description. How are careers made? How does thought change?

Mentors, Elders, Founders, Critics

The National Education Association defines mentoring "as a process in which one person, usually of superior rank, achievement and prestige, guides the development of or sponsors another person, who is seen as the protégé."[16] In the recent Carnegie report on doctoral education,[17] the governing concept was "stewardship," where, to recall a passage quoted in Chapter 2,[18] the steward is one "who will creatively generate new knowledge, critically conserve valuable and useful ideas, and responsibly transform those understandings through writing, teaching, and application."[19] These are welcome words, but they exist on a revealingly high pitch of generality. New knowledge, the conservation of useful ideas, and the responsible transformation of disciplines—these are warmly anodyne notions. They need to be accompanied by recognition of disruption and difficulty. Research on mentorship seems to be growing, and even the relatively small body of systematic writing points to an often fraught relationship.

Reports of doctoral studies across fields include stories of success and flourishing, but also many instances of unrealized, even deeply disappointing mentorship. Faculty can be distant, forgetful, arrogant, or cruel. At least as important is a pervasive unclarity in the relationship. In a recent probing reflection, three historians argued that:

> within the structure of modern graduate education is a medieval institution: the "master" and "apprentice" system of craft education. The model has many virtues but also a very large defect. Under the apprenticeship model, the standard of success is emulation of the mentor, and the essential task of the mentor is replication. The aim of doctoral education, however, is not replication but rather the nurturing of an original creative scholar. Moreover, the old model invites the exercise of overbearing power. In the past such relationships were tolerated, but today they are anachronistic.[20]

Briskly put is David Damrosch's contention that while faculty power "may have eroded in other spheres, it remains decisive when it comes to the training and advising of graduate students."[21] Damrosch concludes that "A reproductive model of mentoring subtly reinforces social as well as intellectual conformity."[22] The passage of academic generations risks arriving at self-stunting impasse in which strong supervisors inhibit the independence of young scholars, or where disenchanted youth loses confidence in wisdom from above.

A paradox that invites the difficulty has been well articulated by Stefan Collini. He notes, in a reflection mentioned earlier,[23] that universities are "among the very few institutions whose rationale includes selecting and shaping their own future staff." Here is continuity. But because the outcome of education is open-ended inquiry, it becomes "a kind of preparation for autonomy" with "more than its share of the paradox involved in *telling* someone to 'be autonomous!'"[24] Indeed, for anyone who has belonged to both sides of the relation, the memory of freedom/dependence and imitation/parody is vivid, if not haunting. It is, after all, an intimate relation, one of the few professional connections that stand close to that between parent and child. No one should be surprised if advice in the Carnegie mode sounds too abstract for the singularity of the couple.

The humanities have a distinctive place within this passage of generations. Because new contributions are so often cast in terms of new interpretations, what's at stake can appear not only as an advance in knowledge, but as an entirely changed way of seeing. The change can be on the relatively small scale—a rereading of Constable's relation to Gainsborough, or the role of Alcibiades' speech in Plato's *Symposium*. But frequently enough, the novelty of interpretation is also a change in tone, an up-to-dateness that implies distance from stodgy work of twenty years ago, or ten, or five. Any glance through the last century will notice the successive intellectual revolutions that have overturned the basic presuppositions of disciplines, one after another. During the last century, every field in the humanities has transformed its methods, enlarged its subject, and reconsidered its foundations—not once but repeatedly. Formalism has yielded to contextualism, existential subjectivity to structuralist system, systematic theory to a-systematic critique, Europe and North America to the rest of the world, men to humans.

By any measure, these (and other) changes have been transformative, to the point where one generation can strike another as more than unhelpful, as antique and overpaid. Dispute among factions, long-term feuds, and even lawsuits are unsettling to departments, though delicious to local newspaper editors. Yet just as striking are the continuities underlying disruption. The century of professionalism has accommodated radical change—not only in subject and method, but in the diversity of faculty and students—and yet we have reason to suspect that Plato and Confucius would recognize the mood and conduct of a seminar room. The privileged voice, the halting but still moving conversation, the mix of seriousness and laughter, the competition mixed with camaraderie, the openness to revision that can overcome stubbornness, the turn of conversation back upon itself, the shared conviction (on the whole) in the value of free inquiry—these persist through other large changes in the disciplines. Then, too, for all the defiance that new thinking can show toward the old, a signal virtue, shown in offices as well as in seminar, is the cross-generational exchange underlying radical shifts in perspective. Those separated by decades in age and chasms in style still find something to say to one another.

*

On a more theoretical plane, Foucault offers a provocation to usual understandings of intellectual change and development. The proposal of "What is an Author?" is that we must enlarge the idea of authorship, must think beyond the limits of personality or *oeuvre*, and toward the authorship of a system of thought. In certain circumstances, "a person can be the author of much more than a book—of a theory, for instance, of a tradition or a discipline within which new books and authors can proliferate."[25] The possibility has always existed. But something new, thinks Foucault, has happened in the modern epoch. Now we have thinkers and texts generating the terms within which others must think and write. An ongoing "discourse" is founded. These authors have "produced not only their own work, but the possibility and the rules of formation of other texts."[26] So Freud and Marx not only composed their signature works (*The Interpretation of Dreams*, *Das Kapital*); they each established "an endless possibility"[27] of more work within their frame. They laid out terms, concepts, relationships that others would sustain and develop. Apart from the works, they invented a discourse; they are "initiators of discursive practice."[28]

The impetus of "What is an Author?," and also its uncertainty, lie in the effort to separate this phenomenon—founding a discourse—from others that seem to resemble it. Why cannot a novelist also be an initiator of a practice? Foucault accepts and answers this question.

A novelist, say Ann Radcliffe, may begin a tradition, say the Gothic, which others will imitate. So those who follow Radcliffe will use the same "characteristic signs, figures, relationships, and structures,"[29] such as the innocent heroine and the threatening castle. But the founders of discourse do more. They generate the opportunity not only for such similarities but also for differences: "They cleared a space for the introduction of elements other than their own, which, nevertheless, remain within the field of a discourse they initiated."[30] A later thinker can diverge from certain ideas and can develop others; these differences are part of what a discourse permits. They are part of what "discourse" means.

What, then, of science? Doesn't it too generate terms and possibilities, rules and procedures, but also openings to change? Yes, concedes Foucault, all true. Galileo initiated a history of experiment of physics, as did Cuvier in biology and Saussure in linguistics. But another difference appears here. In the sciences, the founding act has no special priority; it may have been abundantly fertile; but it has no claim to permanence. As new discoveries and theories are developed, the claims of the revolutionary scientists can be set aside, or forgotten, or simply honored in their obsolescence. Truth is located in the science, not in the ongoing legacy of the originators. But with the "initiators of discursive practice," such as Marx or Freud, the original statements never disappear. Certain claims may no longer be active or productive; new formulations are developed; but everything new still stands in reference to the origin. Change must occur, but unlike the development of science, change always orients itself to the founding theory. The need to "return to the origin"[31] marks the style of thinking as an abiding discourse rather than a developing science.

This strong argument is important to engage, but also right to resist. The history of the humanities, its generationalism, is as complex as Foucault suggests, but complex in still more complex ways. Think, for instance, of those large discipline-defining books that have been touchstones here: in art history, Panofksy's *Studies in Iconology* (1939); in literary study, Frye's *Anatomy of Criticism*; in feminist studies, De Beauvoir's *The Second Sex* (1946); in philosophy, Wittgenstein's *Philosophical Investigations* (1953); in history, Thompson's *The Making of the English Working Class* (1963). Each is a work of intellectual magnitude, widely acknowledged as marking a turning point in a field. Each challenged entrenched concepts and assumptions. Each laid out a new style of thinking, method of research, domain of inquiry.

Yet, these works are originating in ways that resist Foucault's taxonomy and that raise new problems in academic inheritance. For one thing, can any of these texts be said to have initiated a discourse? All won devoted admirers, and, for a time, some imitators. But a signal feature of their after-history is that revision and criticism appeared so soon alongside the admiration. Within half a generation, these texts—like others the reader can recall—entered the play of counter-example and counter-argument. Specific claims were refused, and governing assumptions challenged. Because the works are large and many-sided, they live on impressively. But they neither sustain nor constrain a discourse that must continually look back to them, or place its next steps in reference to their precedent.

This "growing beyond" even defining moments is a feature of the professionalizing humanities. Critique in pursuit of new knowledge is at once a foundational principle and an engrained style, the result of which is that all "discourse" is vulnerable, no matter how monumental its mark and influence. Marx and Freud are good and revealing examples—revealing in part because their works precede the age of academic professionalism. The force of their theories and the ensuing tradition remain strong; many living thinkers still present their convictions by invoking those proper names. But many more, who work within the broad domains (progressive activism and radical philosophy, psychotherapy and its theory), have moved too far to affiliate to the old identity. As time passes, strong concepts will still be quarried. But there comes a point when too much has been surrendered to let us speak of the "same discourse." Both Marxism and psychoanalysis generated branching thought so varied and dense that each prepared for a surpassing of their central terms and their name. One foot in and one out is a reasonable image for the ambiguous movement forward, not just in Foucault's "discourses," but in the evolution of most disciplines.

We should remember, too, that transformational modern thought often develops without talk of founders or the persistence of the founding theory, even when such founders and original theories can be named. Russell and Moore created the terms and methods of analytic philosophy, much as Husserl and Heidegger did within existential phenomenology. Yet neither lineage remains bound by the initial framework. The dominant mode is of a growing body of work, often interested in the strong early philosophy, but unconstrained by backward glancing. New work need not refer to origins as the never-obsolete "primary coordinates." Feminism is another striking case. It too is a body of thought with decisive texts and figures; but feminist theory (and practice) can acknowledge early definitive statements without staying within their "possibilities" and "rules."

The distinction between "normal" and "revolutionary" science, set out in Kuhn's *The Structure of Scientific Revolutions*, is both too strong to be absolute and too perspicuous to discard. In either aspect, it bears closely on the issues of intellectual genealogy raised by Foucault. Kuhn's root idea is that, ordinarily, a science can carry on its standard research without questioning the informing concepts or deep presuppositions— that is, the "paradigm" on which the research protocols are based. But during revolutionary phases, the paradigm comes under challenge at the foundations. If the challenge succeeds (as in the case of Galileo), it requires a complex set of institutional as well as intellectual adjustments, and then normal science will unfold within the new successful paradigm, working with different instruments, concepts, and world pictures. Famously, Kuhn proposed that Galileo saw a pendulum where Aristotle saw a falling stone and that "after discovering oxygen Lavoisier worked in a different world."[32] Before and after the revolutionary break, scientists lived, not just with different facts, but within "incommensurable" worlds. In the new epoch, normal science resumes, solving the puzzles set out by the new paradigm.

Whether we can speak of truly "incommensurable" world pictures, whether scientific change is ever so total and thoroughgoing, whether "paradigm" is too schematic and reductive a concept—these questions have been continuously debated during the half-century since Kuhn's book was published. But even a rough and ready version of the contrast between normal and revolutionary periods captures something distinctive in the academic humanities, where the onward movement, I've suggested, tends not merely toward novelty but toward astonishment. Indeed, what resembles "normal science" in the humanities, the extension of a theory to another new scene of interpretation (say, a Lacanian reading of Berlioz) is not only undervalued but often the target of special reproach. It will be seen as "mere application" or "entirely predictable." It's not that work must always make a revolution, but "unpredictability" is indeed a virtue. The question of disciplinary change in the humanities continually resists the founder-generated stability of Foucault's "discourses"—an issue that becomes pointed in the press toward interdisciplinarity. It's on this subject that the chapter will end, but only after it encounters a parallel and contrasting problem met on home computers.

Haley's *Roots*: Finding the Threads

Within the realm of the everyday humanities, there are evident analogies to the passage of academic generations. In the practices considered earlier—in living history, for instance, or in book clubs—a relation between elders and novices is a visible element within the community. Newcomers are usually welcome, but they can also be irritating. While the academic world attempts, not always successfully, to map the stages of initiation and to indicate benchmarks of success and promotion, the informal associations tend toward implicit, sometimes awkward marks of entry and belonging. In the present chapter, though, the emphasis falls on a specific turn in the question of seniority and youth. What happens when the tie is not just to a previous generation or two, but to all generations, no matter how distant the reach? What's at stake in the practice of amateur genealogy?

The development has been widespread, significant, interesting, and understudied. Since the later 1970s, especially in the English-speaking world, the commitment to private family history has spread in a series of waves. First came the publication of Alex Haley's *Roots* in 1976 to spectacular popular success, and then, recently, developments in genomics and digital technology. By the end of the millennium, home researchers with an Internet connection and a few surnames could expect the rapid sprouting of a family tree.

Literary histories of the 1970s typically emphasize the rise and spread of postmodernism. Within any broader cultural view, however, Haley's *Roots* was the landmark text, the work that offered family history as central vocation. That the hyphen in African-American marks more than one separation; that accompanying the violent passage from Africa to North American slavery was the violence of broken historical continuity; that slavery coerced lives toward a perpetual present: Haley drew *Roots* from these deep implications. Writing in the first decade after the civil rights legislation of the middle sixties, he brought the consolation, and exhilaration, of long temporality. The immediate impact, of course, was felt within an African-American community that recognized a new way to reclaim identity. Other groups followed in short order.

Early in the text, Kunta Kinte explains the attractions of ancestry to his younger brother Lamin:

> "Our father's brothers are also the sons Kairaba Kunta Kinte, for whom I am named," said Kunta proudly. "But our uncles Janneh and Saloum were born of Sireng," he said. Lamin looked puzzled, but Kunta kept on explaining. "Sireng was our grandfather's first wife, who died before he married our Grandma Yaisa." Kunta arranged twigs on the ground to show the Kinte family's different individuals.[33]

The family tree designed from twigs is an animating image of the work. It suggests that even distant ancestors were gazing back toward distant ancestors and that self-understanding depends on grasping a web of kin.

Anyone who spends some time in the pages of recent private genealogy finds Haley everywhere. He is often explicitly celebrated. But whether his name is spoken or not, the influence of *Roots* continues unabated. Before all else, it epitomized a project of identity-making that came to pervade a growing group of curious and committed amateurs. To have a self, strong and abundant, was to have a lengthening past of distant selves. For a full generation now, crossing the cusp of the millennium, families have busily deepened their pasts, with an emotional valence almost always positive.

The Nicholson-Rauch family (Luzerne County, Pennsylvania) speaks in unembarrassed collective affirmation on its introductory page:

> No family could be prouder of its roots than we are. We believe they are important to us because of the sacrifices they made for us and the lessons we can learn from them, for after all, they are a part of us. We are indebted to them for their courage and fortitude, their forthrightness, their faith and their sense of

character. We are dedicated to identifying as many as possible, learning everything we can about them, making each one more than a name, a date and a place and leaving that record as a legacy to their courage. We want to build memories of the past for the children of the future.[34]

Condensed in these direct words are attitudes seen in many similar ventures, above all, the resonance of continuity. The "We" of the current generation tends to recede under the weight of admiration for the ancestors and hopes for the successors. To live in the genealogical present is to assume the burden of inquiry as recompense for an accumulating past. Identity appears as an effect of the generational unfolding: many projects take pleasure in seeing how habits and predilections from centuries ago seem to live on through family time. It's as if value emanates from the past, while the power of consciousness is the gift and responsibility of the present.

There is, after all, some good reason for the heroizing attitudes toward forebears. Many genealogies are prompted by broken connections caused by economic emigration, political flight, or religious exile. Those who left old worlds in pursuit of new confronted many difficulties, only some of which can be retrieved. But there's enough indication of risk and danger to warrant the admiring rhetoric, rarely interrupted by critique. Furthermore, a condition of the research is that in the backward movement of time, the number of ancestors grows quickly, while the number of documents and relics seem to diminish at the same rate. It becomes very difficult to develop a picture of more than a few who lived before the eighteenth century. This means that, to a significant extent, genealogy is the study of life under modernity. The Irish diaspora, the settlement of Australia, the frontier movements in the United States, the after-effects of revolution in Russia—these have been threshold events in the expanding universe of family history.

Legends and Scandals of Ancestry: Celebration, Shame, Critique

The romance of genealogy, abounding in the ardor of the prose, is nurtured on distance in space as well as time. The travel back to home in the old country or the discovery of time-encrusted relics partake of what Benjamin describes as the "aura" of an object, "its presence in time and space, its unique existence at the place where it happens to be."[35] Many genealogies describe these physical encounters and also the inner reveries that they stir. You need to be made of stone to miss the emotion quickened by recovery of a forgotten remnant from the past: a photo, a hairbrush, a cup, a coat. Gray's "Elegy" gives an archetype of melancholy reflection launched by drifting thought in front of a relic. But melancholy, as in Gray, is mixed with soaring fantasy, fed by the hopes of more and older finds.

The arithmetic can surprise anyone who hasn't made the calculations. Simply go back 250 years, and then count the number of ancestors who lived those few generations ago. The figure quickly passes 500. Not only is it a dizzying number for any close act of historical recovery, but it also prepares for a favorite feature article of bored editors. With so many intersecting lines of cousinship, distant lives—politically distant, racially distant—will quickly weave together. In the spring of 2015, the front page of *The Guardian* splashed the news that "Benedict Cumberbatch will pay tribute to his late second cousin 16 times removed when he reads a poem at the reburial of Richard III in Leicester Cathedral."[36] The paper then noted how "It is estimated that between one and 17 million people in the UK alone are related in some way to the Plantagenet king, but Cumberbatch's kinship is much closer than most." As Steven Pinker has caustically observed, it is "mathematical necessity, not a surprise, that genealogy will turn up strange bedfellows."[37] But, then, the recurrent fascination in the media suggests that popular interest in tales of surprising descent never wanes. For those pursuing their own genealogies, appetite is undiminished by the mathematics.

Haley came to call *Roots* a work of "faction." The word is part concession, part assertion. Despite his many laborious acts of historical recovery, the book never conceals the openly fictive quality of its scene-setting, its character-drawing, and the reconstruction of its events. From its opening, the narrative enters the consciousness of long-dead ancestors and recounts events from a perspective that only a participant could experience. It does so without hesitation or pretense. The effect is a constant movement between recoverable and irrecoverable history. Haley thanks his research collaborator, his friend

George Sims, who pored "through volumes by the hundreds, and other kinds of documents by the thousands." Research provides the "historical and cultural material" that Haley has "woven around the lives of the people in this book."[38]

The skilful "weaving" of context around nuggets of detail won *Roots* millions of readers and scores of detractors. It also established the mixed paradigm of the amateur genealogy it stimulated. On one side, you find the restrained austerity of exact detail. Proven records of kinship are produced with proud clarity: dates and places of birth, marriage, and death recorded with no context, no weaving. Elsewhere, though, appear unquenchable efforts to construct connecting links that might sustain an ongoing narrative, as much desired as vexed. The more formal sponsors of genealogy guard against lax specula-tion, but there can be no stopping the interested parties. Countless examples on the Internet move from pleasure in the recovery of fact toward the evocation of continuity through generations and the emotional meanings of story. Yet these hopes confront the hard docu-mentary truth: that except in the rarest of cases, genealogy leaves its table of ancestry cluttered with absent boxes, and traffics in hypothesis, surmise, and speculation. It relies on Haley's "faction," an acceptance of the need to move beyond bare objectivity in order to imagine the truth, including large historical truth. Scant details of immigration from Ireland to England, or from Italy to the United States, invoke a broad course of social change. Take this engaging and instructive sequence from the first page of the Keene and Phillips genealogy:

> The Kershners and most of the rest of our German branch immigrated to Pennsylvania from German speaking lands in the period of about 1730–1750. This was a time of great economic and religious upheaval in Germany. Some of these families may have come to obtain religious freedom but others undoubtedly came because of the economic devastation in their homelands. Some of the families associated with the Kershners are Fryberger, Hass and Geis. Once in Pennsylvania, these families obtained land from the Penn family and turned to farming. They were all (as far as I know) of the Reformed or Lutheran persuasion. They all lived in Berks County, mostly in the north-west quadrant.

The Keene (or Kühn as it was originally spelled) family came to America more recently, having emigrated from Toba, a tiny town in the principality of Schwarzburg-Sondershausen to Pennsylvania in 1852. The period of around 1848–52 was a time of renewed emigration from Germany as it coincided with the failure of a popular revolution there, the Märzrevolution. I don't know if the Keene family was involved at all in that revolution but in any case they chose that time to move to Reading, Pa., perhaps along with some of their compatriots. We know of at least one fellow townsman who came to Reading at about the same time. The Keenes became a mining and manufacturing family. We have very little information about one of our German family branches, the Snyders, who married into the Keene family. When we first pick up their trail in about 1840, they were a family of hatters, also living in Reading.[39]

The Keene/Phillips passages follow a pattern appearing in many works. A line of ancestry stretches a cord of relationship through decades and centuries. But the mere confirmation of lineage is rarely enough; so the lives of forebears are inserted within a broader history (the "time of great economic and religious upheaval in Germany" which leads on to "the failure of a popular revolution"). A linguistic device in these paragraphs appears regularly, the resources of "Some" and "some." Dealing with not only numerous but also highly varied lives, the genealogists need to find expression for the clarity and obscurity in the past. "Some"/"some" is a comfortable principle for sorting populations that quickly rival small villages in size.

The leading sites of the new genealogy are the United States and Australia, two nations that routinely furnish affirmative images of immigration and settlement. The stories of many families are told as triumphs over hardship, heroic struggles with social and natural adversity. The record of long journey, early death, a lineage surviving even as it dwindles in size—these constructions can be drawn, persuasively drawn, from the limited recoveries. But, of course, the two countries are also notorious sites of unchosen arrival. Slaves and convicts occupy places in the genealogical table, uncomfortable places for those pursuing ancestral boosterism. Formal genealogy, after all, began as an opportunity to display the ornamental past of the peerage, to claim high and distant origin; it can still be used to solidify family eminence and pride. On the other hand, as events in both Austrialia and the U.S. have shown, a thorough history can undo the claims of purity in a single stroke.

The recent televisual career of Henry Louis Gates, Jr. has achieved its resonance within this context. In 2006, Gates launched a four-episode PBS miniseries called *African American Lives*, which in its first season recovered the ancestry of some well-known celebrities, including Quincy Jones, Whoopi Goldberg, and Oprah Winfrey. Two years later, another four episodes appeared (Maya Angelou, Tina Turner, Morgan Freeman, among others). Moving within the encouraging path marked by *Roots*, the show was a double gesture of repair and assertion, which gave its African-American participants the dignity of lengthening and complex history. A connecting thread was Gates's own ancestry, retrieved as the series unfolded.

In 2010 came a successor series, *Faces of America*, also on PBS, which moved across lines of ethnicity to trace the ancestry of twelve well-known Americans (including Meryl Streep, Mike Nichols, and Queen Noor of Jordan). Then in 2012 came a significant expansion with *Finding Your Roots*, which continues up to the time of this writing. Again, episodes begin with an account of the guests' achievements and distinction in music, in politics, in media. There follow the surprises borne by the professional staff—the tracing of documents, the findings through analysis of DNA—taking the story back as far as possible and creating the uncanny sensation of identity defamiliarized through the elongations of time. Sameness and otherness dance awkwardly.

Freud's reflections on "family romance,"[40] the fantasy of replacing one's actual parents with grander and more powerful ones, illuminate some of the yearning in the narratives, the pleasure of connection to braver, larger pioneers who made possible the comfortable settlements of the present day. But the logic of research—the blunt record of evidence that cannot be romanced away—can quickly corrode a vaunting pride. In the first episode of *Finding Your Roots*, Harry Connick, Jr., one of the principal guests, is made to discover uncomfortable connections to the Civil War, namely that his great-great-grandfather, though he didn't own slaves, enlisted in the Confederate army and served for three years:

Harry was crushed. I reminded him that he wasn't responsible for his ancestors' actions, but still he felt ashamed. "To hear it for the first time, you would hope that your ancestor would have been working with Harriet Tubman or something, trying to help as many people. The fact that he's a private in the Confederacy—it's not like he tried it for six months and said, 'You know what, man? This isn't for me.'"

Wrestling with this news, Harry tried to make sense of it all. "The fact that he didn't own slaves, does that mean he just didn't have any money and he was too young? I'm grasping to try to rationalize."[41]

The semi-spectacular controversy of a few years later came out of this capacity of genealogy to produce apparent moral stain. Gates became entangled in an attempt to suppress details of Ben Affleck's ancestry, precisely the slave-owning history that Harry Connick, Jr. had dreaded. An Affleck episode was aired in the fall of 2014 (with no mention of slave-holding); then a few months later, emails released by WikiLeaks showed that the actor had exerted pressure to suppress the painful facts (" 'I didn't want any television show about my family to include a guy who owned slaves,' Mr. Affleck wrote on Facebook") and that Gates had discussed censorship with a Sony executive.[42] The show was suspended, but then allowed to resume at the beginning of 2016.

A minor media-driven scandal, but one that unveils the critical force that lies within the genealogical imperative. Part of the gentle polemic of Gates's television career has been to weaken claims of racial purity and family essence. The guest alongside Harry Connick, Jr. was Branford Marsalis, who became an exemplary subject/object of destabilizing genealogy: "He had embarked on this journey with us with very few preconceived notions about his ancestry and was willing to part with them when necessary." When Gates asks what Marsalis thinks about the "sense of self" retrieved through ancestry, he gives the answer that fits the work of critique: "I think my DNA, as you explained it to me, makes me receptive, a lot more receptive to differences in people as opposed to the people who cling to similarities."[43] Gates and his show resist the cult of the same, genealogy as the elaboration of pedigree; they offer the self as a fiber of many strands, incapable of sustaining its purity through many backward generations.

As part of the media spark, Gates displayed the information retrieved from his own genome, revealing 50 percent European ancestry.[44]

Gates, Jr.'s series have drawn on a persistent appeal in the genealogical renaissance, the making of the self interpreted as an essentially historical project. The task is set for each: a committed labor to set individuality within a web of ancestry, to accept surprises along the way, even the shattering ones, and then to assert the changed sense of identity. Genealogy becomes a contemporary rite of initiation; the possession of a long life in time can accompany, or even substitute for, life in space: a small dwelling may house the descendant of heroic lineage. As Zerubavel emphasizes, "the ways in which we are related to our ancestors and relatives have come to constitute the fundamental templates we also use to conceptualize other forms of relatedness, as genealogy has clearly become the predominant framework within which we now think about relatedness in general."[45] And not simply relatedness but personhood. For a growing audience and an increasing number of practitioners, self-understanding becomes inseparable from these links to the past. What gives added force to the idea is that increasingly the identity project is not a product of reality-refusing fantasy, but the result of "scientific" technique and professionally sanctioned procedures. The televised magic in *Finding Your Roots* depends on surprises founded on the new science, which duly astonish the guests who learn all that family history can now determine.

History from Below

The spectacular success of Haley's *Roots*, as book and on television, and the significant viewership of Gates, Jr.'s series, have secured a continuing interest and a large audience. But their visibility shouldn't obscure the bustle of popular genealogy beyond industrial-scale media. For most of the many people laboring to construct family history, even those comfortably in the middle class, resources are limited. Without network contracts, professional advice, or the cash value of celebrity, the everyday genealogist works under constraint. The revolution in technology has been the indispensable context; words of praise are often directed to the software packages that have enabled the search. It's by no means cost-free, this vocation. It requires time, a reasonable Internet connection, often a subscription to a service like ancestry.com, and sometimes the capacity to travel distances to find a document, a gravestone, or a house. Still, though the investment is significant, many millions of people can, and choose to, make it.

Consider that it's only one generation old, the new genealogy. In the 1980s and early 1990s, records were scattered and largely uncatalogued, deposited in uncoordinated offices and local libraries, and only formally gathered in a few major repositories that required time-consuming negotiation to penetrate. The committed searchers relied on magazines and books published for a niche audience. Then rapidly at the start of the millennium, technology created a qualitative change. Now, working on their own initiative, individuals could discover biological connection, an activity that has begun to occur on a large scale. Most recently, a consumer-grade DNA test (requiring only a sample of spit) not only accelerates proof of kinship, but also becomes an instrument for the analysis of a family's health profile. In the summer of 2015, ancestry.com launched AncestryHealth. The firm's advantage lies not in biological science but in the sheer size of its database; at the time of this writing, ancestry.com holds over 16 billion records.

On the high corporate end, money grows on the family trees. It stimulates corporate organization, new scientific method, and active marketing. It draws upon and extends the protocols devised by earlier researchers, especially the Church of Jesus Christ of Latter-Day Saints. As Julia Watson has well observed, those with authority often lay down dicta of appropriate procedure and tone. The official guides emphasize objectivity, and the need to resist narrative and imagination: "A personal story is subordinated to the history of the family, and that story tolerates no embroidery."[46] For Watson, these attitudes confirm the essentially "conservative" nature of genealogy as such, in contrast to the rights of subjectivity claimed by autobiography.

In the informal expanding universe of amateur discovery, however, the resistance to formality is often a badge of honor. A cursory glance at the sprawl of records shows endless variety in presentation. Photo libraries, personal notes, bibliography, and links, speculations on the temperament of an ancestor, self-conscious reflections on the task at hand—all circulate beyond the reach of discipline or calls to objectivity. Frequently, the compositors will admit to deficiency—an impasse in a line of descent, say, or a failure to confirm a birth site, or a dependence on open guesswork—but shruggingly. "This is what I've found. This is how I present it." The result is a disorganized and dispersed collective history which has often irritated professional historians. Private genealogists are largely indifferent to questions of theory and method; they don't assume that a course in historiography is prerequisite to their work. That they are nevertheless so many means that they are visible in the archive, and even when they win no respect from professionals, they come to rely on one another.

The work of genealogy, in spite of the personal and private aims in which it begins, has become a vast spontaneous community discovering itself with speed and pleasure. It grows, first, from the necessary intersection of separate lines of recovery. Early in the work comes recognition that separate questers are searching for the same clue, that my great-great-great-grandfather is also yours and yours and yours. This biological relatedness is no more important than the research collaboration that the work also stimulates. Because searching is endless and arduous, it follows a staccato rhythm, as a quest happens on a significant find and then dries up for many months. During periods of impasse, little is more welcome than contributions arriving out of someone else's research along different family branches; in a digital age, new discoveries can be quickly shared. Requests for such help are common, as in these lines from the Nicholson-Rauch page: "Please feel free to browse our site. Look carefully through the names. Let us know if any are familiar. We share here—all that we have. We would like your suggestions and additions." Such ceremonies of mutual gratitude have become familiar. As the practice grows (and grows), the social webbing becomes at once wider and denser.

The result is that projects beginning in narrow spheres of known family relations can scarcely avoid overcoming that close privacy as forgotten ties show themselves. Nothing is formalized, but the pooling of knowledge tends toward a gently self-regulating community. Words of impatience appear but rarely. Is it too much to speak of the accidental ethics of the new genealogy? An ethics built on exchange, openness, humility, gratitude—affirmations based on nothing more than tacit codes of understanding? A sign of the developing reciprocity is a change from the burnishing of pedigree to the acceptance of undistinguished ancestry, hybrid lineage, and shameful precursors alongside the heroic and resolute. Genealogy still often begins, as critics point out, with the prideful assertion of a family treasure; an enthusiast in the circle of cousins unearths a birth certificate or a forgotten photograph; warm nostalgic smiles are exchanged. But as searching continues, on a scale only recently made possible, then connections are made to those with unknown surnames in different regions, classes, races. It's what Gates, Jr.'s show most informatively proves: that just a few steps down the ladder of descent reveal that it's not a ladder at all, but an intricate reticulation, branches wrapped around other branches, and then others still. Against Watson's view of genealogy as the conservative pursuit of social eminence, Catherine Nash persuasively argues that personal genealogies "map out complicated geographies of migration, origins and belonging, sometimes reproducing, sometimes subverting the language of cultural purity, fundamentalism and essentialism."[47] To take this still emerging activity as seriously as it deserves is to recognize it as a significant practice, maturing with unknown consequences.

*

Historians have been slow to pay genealogy that serious regard. The uncredentialed trawl through archives, the personal and emotive cast of the research, and the indifference to rigorous procedure have made the work appear little more than hobby or crotchet. Graeme Davison, a leading Australian historian, satirized his country's pursuit of private genealogy in biting terms. It appealed, he suggested, mostly to women, the middle-aged and well-to-do, and to the "old Protestant Australia, which, arguably, has been most threatened by the changes of the postwar era."[48] The genealogical field, he writes, is "a private or tribal one that connects only tenuously with the concerns of national or international history" and from the perspective of a professional historian, its precipitates "may appear not only trivial but almost inscrutable": "plotless, disconnected, unselective...It speaks not to our sense of historical significance, but to our need for personal identity."[49] Davison accompanied this polemic with challenging words in an essay entitled "Speed-Relating." Tanya Evans offered a counterposition, beginning with reminders of the high disdain found in the academy—"Family historians have been dismissed by professional and academic historians, in Australia and beyond, as 'misty-eyed and syrupy' and their findings and practices deemed irrelevant to the wider historical community"—and then arguing that the challenge from family history is deeper than first appears and important to meet honestly.[50] Especially in Australia, family history is where the "pioneer" myth has been contested, because "so many family trees provide evidence of convict and/or Aboriginal ancestry."[51] Further, argues Evans, while colonial history has been unfashionable in the universities, "genealogists remain fervently and intensely interested in that period."[52]

The question raises telling issues in the relation between academic and everyday humanities. Many historians have kept a high-minded distance from the ardent genealogists occupying too many seats in the public records room. More interesting are the attempts to traverse the distance, and here Graeme Davison's career opens a path for thought. Not long after his snippy sexist satire of middle-aged well-to-do women sketching tables of descent and the broad comedy of ancestor pursuit, Davison found himself practicing and defending the ludicrous art. In *Lost Relations: Fortunes of My Family in Australia's Golden Age* (2015) he turns the experience of a long academic career to the recovery of his own family history, setting out in duly rueful tones: "I did not get far along the road before realising that family history is a very different pursuit from academic history, my day job. It is not a search for general historical truth but a quest for personal identity."[53] The turn to the personal brings admission of his past disdain:

> For most of my life I have avoided family history. The crowds of chattering genealogists in public libraries and archives are one of the daily hazards of the academic researcher. I have written critically about the perils of 'speed-relating,' the craze for online genealogy, and the business activities of Ancestry.com and the other commercial genealogical websites.[54]

The result is a book-length account of Davison's ancestors—caught in photos, relics, letters—as they move from Britain to Australia and beget Davison himself, the academic historian who has "succumbed to the appeal of family history."[55] But he is also insistent that more is in question than identity, that such work can make links between domestic and private history. This is a point that Tanya Evans has developed further, arguing that it's now past time to "to reassess the condescension shown towards the motivations, methods and findings of family historians as some innovative Australian historians have begun to do."[56] She finds examples of an emerging reconciliation, where the long personal labors of family historians are not only acknowledged but turned to urgent use, breaking up assumptions—about the solidity of histories of the family, power between men and women, nation and empire.

This book's proposition remains that subject matter defines a discipline, while method establishes a credential. It has close bearing on the case of genealogy, which like the example of *Wikipedia*, shows the humanities moving in and out of the university. Evans writes generously of exchanges between historians and family historians, even as she holds that while amateurs can provide details and fill some "gaps left by 'official' history," it is for academic practitioners to give form to the "content." She notes that "Professional organizations such as SAG [Society of Australian Genealogists] ... encourage family historians to be consistent in the manner in which they conduct their research and to standardize their recorded discoveries so that more people can access and use it."[57]

All this is fair, persuasive, and just. Still, a challenge remains, one that involves more than the challenge of content fallen through the gaps in the academic record. More fundamental is the indifference of the genealogists to the "representative case." Not only in history as discipline, but throughout the disciplines of the humanities, the representative example holds an anchoring position. Argument and narrative consistently rest on assumptions of how particularity (particular lives, texts, paintings, scores, events, moral or grammatical intuitions) becomes exemplary. What would the humanities be without reliance on the representative and the exemplary, on acts of generalization and abstraction that establish at minimum some wider implication and more ambitiously some pattern or regularity or rule?

Amateur genealogy, in one respect, confirms the particularizing mission of academic history that proudly resists the abstractions of neighboring disciplines. But genealogy carries the banner to the furthest extreme. For most practitioners, the particular is all, the specific ancestors, curios, travel routes, wedding days, pursued with full indifference to any representative quality or broader meaning. "Interpretation" counts far less than mere recovery. When Davison speaks of his *Lost Relations* as "a quest for personal identity" rather than a "general historical truth,"[58] he catches the contrast. It's not that genealogy is individual or solipsistic. As I've suggested, the new digital techniques open surprising affiliations and extended networks of collaboration. But even the strong social character of the work remains founded on (and warranted by) "personality," whose claim depends on nothing more or less than the facts of specific ancestry.

The prospect of collaboration between academic history and private genealogy is promising. But as Evans describes and imagines it, the weight of significance remains on the academic side, its experience and its methods, which should respect, but also tutor, the energy of domestic researchers. The vision is plausible, tested, and near. Yet it misses the strongest and most interesting challenge from the independent laptoppers, namely just this refusal of the usual purposes of public history. The commitment of genealogy to absolute specificity, those lives connected to our lives, can bring more information to the historian, but they will surely bring too much, details too copious to assimilate in a proper history. They are experts too, the amateur genealogists, but experts in a defiantly singular domain.

In the difficulty lies the virtue. A better arrangement would be one closer to the condition emerging now. Academic history will lose some disdain and will draw on the work of amateur genealogists to refine the subfield of family history; a small but significant number of those amateurs will refine their methods to meet the standards found in universities, coming under the tutelage of professional historians ready to collaborate. But a far larger group will carry on without refinement or credential, stimulated by a "personal" curiosity unencumbered by scruples of method. These last will never fit comfortably into standardly published histories. Most of their work will, and must, remain outside the norms of acceptable research, but in remaining there, they will help to mark a limit.

Not a happy marriage or tactful reconciliation between the academic and everyday humanities, but a growing exchange that also measures the distance between them. It is right to preserve/extend the experience of generations of professionals, right to open the walled garden to knowledge sprouting outside, and also right to embrace the inassimilable value of the recovery of singular lives, justified by nothing more than that they lived. One significant good is indeed the widening reach of professional historians, their acknowledgment and training of some few private seekers. But an equal good will be the ever-growing ardent labor of those who are uninterested in, perhaps unsuited to, academic projects, who remain confidently incommensurable.

*

These uneasy and altering relations between scholars and independents also offer a small case study of the disciplines in time. A resistance toward private genealogists transmutes into acknowledgement. As the findings of amateurs are quarried, they become materials within a disciplinary event already in train, the development of family history as a growing subfield with all the relevant professional apparatus (conferences, journals, etc.). Apart from its own rich content, the sequence raises again a question of interdisciplinarity, which is itself a temporal event, a motion of intellectual life out of one structure of knowledge and into another. This chapter began by invoking issues of inheritance and transmission; it's in those terms that we can resume thought about the interdisciplinary.

The Disciplines in Time: Branching and Forking

Alongside the word "global," "interdisciplinary" sounds as the recurrent piety in mission statements of colleges and universities. What does it mean? Any definition is ugly, but this one will be over in a sentence. Interdisciplinarity, according to Béchillon's fair statement, is "a way of fitting together bodies of knowledge that leads to ongoing partial reorganization of existing theoretical fields, as if through dialogue."[59] Harmless but nearly vacuous, these phrases remind us that to call for "interdisciplinarity" *as such* is to make a demand too general to meet—or to fail to meet. As a chant, it is contentless. Which disciplines? Bound by what "inter?" In practice, it suggests any work drawing concepts from more than one lineage, brought together "as if through dialogue." Inevitably, the call attracts a rejoinder, just as pious: namely, that there can be no interdisciplinarity without initial mastery of one discipline. An unnamed professor at Emory made the familiar point on the university's website: "in this breakthrough [to] interdisciplinarity, we are losing track of the notion of discipline. It's important to remember that interdisciplinarity can only exist if there are disciplines."[60] But, then, of course, academic disciplines, especially in the humanities, are already concatenations of interests. A single discipline not only includes different subjects, but increasingly different methods. Historical approaches; theoretical elaborations; varieties of close reading; acts of preservation, cataloguing, and editing; digital processing and archiving; these among others register a dispersal of concerns resisting definition by discipline, much as they put strains on the work of named departments. Acts of crossing are just as frequent between subfields as across fields, and to traverse the length of a discipline is to cover distances as great as many a "leap" across the interdisciplinary boundary.

A recent mission statement affirms "Interdisciplinary Studies" as "a recognized and growing set of ideas, practices, and organizations. The interdisciplinary studies program (INTS) at the University of Texas at Arlington enables students to build rigorous and coherent personalized degree plans guided by professional advisors."[61] The bland words reveal a central tension. On one side stands the familiar excited call to join the growing wave of interdisciplinary research. On the other comes recognition that study must be "personalized." As long as the campaign remains abstract and contentless, this is the inevitable doubleness. A marking feature of cross-field work in the humanities is that interdisciplinary work, even of the most exciting kind, is nearly always interdisciplinary in its own way. Great achievement—such as, for instance, the philosopher Bernard Williams writing on Greek tragedy—can be as fully admirable as inimitable. This, and any other major work you're likely to recall, may inspire, but is unlikely to serve as paradigm for a new research domain or as an example of new method. It's far too singular for that. Nor should the singularity be surprising. As strong thinkers leave one region of inquiry to encounter part of another, the pathways are likely to be sharply distinct, perhaps compelling but most often *sui generis*.

A real need has been masked by an administrative slogan. For the humanities, as for the wider university, the need to keep knowledge moving is paramount. This chapter began with the fifteenth-century recovery of ancient texts and the act of transmission as the condition of inquiry—a question of inheritance and also mentorship. But if we also keep in mind the task of genealogy, then it's clear that the quest for interdisciplinarity involves a problem in ancestry. In every discussion of new cross-field research, the conundrum of lineage returns. How can those in old fields, the parent disciplines, properly assess work born of two (or more) parents? As long as the research remains so individual ("personalized"), the difficulties are unanswerable. As one informant put it not long ago, "Interdisciplinarity is a luxury of seniority."[62]

How might we think of it more usefully? In the realm of software it happens that groups of developers may begin to disagree about the evolution of the project. Negotiation then ensues, and when successful, the different branches remain within the overarching structure given by the source code. However, when differences cannot be reconciled, a "forking" occurs. This is the name now given to developments that have become so mismatched, either in detail or in governing concept, that no reassimilation is possible. At that point the fork occurs. The resistant community breaks off and conducts its work according to its own lights, with no obligation to meet the goals of the original group, or even to maintain relations with it.

"Forking" has been a charged issue in software circles. It's often seen as both a technical and a social failure. Where an ongoing venture might have been conducted by a stable working group, a break has occurred that can seem an unnecessary duplication, the product of bloody-minded obsessiveness or of mere rivalry and jealousy. The hacker dictionary observes that forking:

> is considered a Bad Thing not merely because it implies a lot of wasted effort in the future, but because forks tend to be accompanied by a great deal of strife and acrimony between the successor groups over issues of legitimacy, succession, and design direction. There is serious social pressure against forking. As a result, major forks (such as the Gnu-Emacs/XEmacs split, the fissionings of the 386BSD group into three daughter projects, and the short-lived GCC/EGCS split) are rare enough that they are remembered individually in hacker folklore.

The remark appears in a recent essay on the history of forking, which collects hundreds more cases where an apparently coherent project severed and separated.[63] It should stand alongside Larry Sanger's barbed comment, when he became dismayed at *Wikipedia*'s turn from academic authority: "I do not see how there can *not* be a more academic fork of the project in the future."[64]

"Forking" offers an illuminating mirror to the problem of generational change in the academy, and especially to the question of interdisciplinarity. It helps clarify the distinction between bravura acts of individual cross-field thinking (Thompson, Butler, Wollheim, and many others) and the emergence of new fields. The act of drawing on concepts or evidence from another domain, even a "faraway" domain, can be ill-considered, risky, or prodigious, but it's by no means uncommon. The phrase "Here I borrow an idea from" and its ilk have a long history. They can open to works of remarkable inventiveness (Foucault on Velázquez's "Las Meninas"), which we can happily but uselessly call interdisciplinary. All fields of knowledge are seamed on every side, in their depth as well as breadth. A plunge deep into art history can land in the pool of linguistics. An analysis of eighteenth-century texts arrives at twenty-first century software coding. The study of musical performance finds itself within gender theory. These moves are no longer surprising; they may open or close eyes; but they are now part of the routine of work *within disciplines*, part of its normal science. In undramatic ways, to carry on within discipline is to be alert to the applications and appropriations of ideas from across the seam. In the language of software development, these are nothing like "forks"; they are branches on the same tree.

The advantage of the analogy is that it shows the complexity of *descent* in intellectual life. There is the expected branching in many different directions, but all acceptable as part of continuous labor within a discipline. But then there is the fork. No thank you, we intend to follow our own course; we wish you well (enough); but we now work under our new name with a membership that shouldn't be confused with yours. Here is the birth of Gender Studies, African-American Studies, American Studies, Media Studies, and so on. Like "the fissionings of the 386BSD group into three daughter projects," small groups form into new communities, which in the academic world take the aspect of new centers or institutes, new programs or departments.

Suppose we think less about interdisciplinarity as an achievement in intellectual space, the crossing of boundaries between separate fields of inquiry—though, of course, it is partly that. But suppose we retain the image of intellectual genealogy and generations, the emergence of new problems/concepts/methods that for a time seem branches of the old tree, but that sometimes become a sharper fork—a break into new coherence, new institutional life. The ambiguity of generation is inbuilt. Is American Studies a new discipline or a new focus within existing disciplines? At what point do the digital humanities mark out a field rather than a collection of tools? Should faculty in the Study of Women and Gender only have appointments in already existing fields or in a department of their own? These are always uneasy questions, but if feelings can be soothed, they are also productive ones.

What the forking analogy suggests is that the crucial issue is never purely intellectual or individual, never given simply by a new problem, which can almost always be grafted on to an old discipline. The telling point is whether a group of researchers, across or *within* departments, understand their interests separately, or separately enough, to warrant a new research program. When it succeeds, it will be accepted as new knowledge and new institutional presence. It needn't succeed. As in the branches of family ancestry, the genealogical table of disciplines contains empty boxes where a line is extinct. And yet it would be hard to argue that the last century of academic thought hasn't gained from the multiplication of disciplines. Of course, it brings growing pain, budget rivalry, intellectual consternation. But it's not only good for a new domain of knowledge to grow; it has bracing effects on the "parent" disciplines, forcing them to reconsider boundaries and first principles.

Within the conventions of Open Source Software, the threat of forking is always at hand. One of the "four freedoms" is precisely "The freedom to study how the program works, and change it so it does your computing as you wish."[65] Universities are not quite like that. But they could usefully come closer. Instead of calling for interdisciplinarity as an abstract virtue, universities should think more in terms of intellectual–collaborative–institutional developments. When small groups are forming, watch and encourage. Provide facilities, time, and money. Expect mostly branches but some forks.

Notes

1. Stephen Greenblatt, *The Swerve: How the World Became Modern* (New York: Norton, 2011).
2. Vespasiano da Bisticci, *Renaissance Princes, Popes, and Prelates*, tr. William George and Emily Waters (New York Harper & Row, 1963), 332.
3. Ibid., 397.

4. Jacob Burckhardt, *The Civilization of the Renaissance in Italy*, tr. S. G. C. Middlemore, vol. 1 (London: Macmillan and Co., 1904), 220.

5. Ibid., 102.

6. Ibid., 102.

7. Alfred North Whitehead, *Process and Reality*, ed. David Ray Griffin and Donald W. Sherburne (New York: The Free Press, 1978), 39.

8. Burckhardt, *Civilization of the Renaissance*, 272.

9. Ibid., 281.

10. Ibid., 276.

11. Ibid., 3.

12. James Boswell, *The Life of Samuel Johnson*, ed. George Birkbeck Hill (New York: Bigelow, Brown, 1921), 389.

13. Samuel Johnson, "Proposals for Printing the Dramatic Works of William Shakespeare," *The Works of Samuel Johnson*, (London: F.C. and J. Rivington, 1823), 129.

14. Ibid., 177.

15. Eviatar Zerubavel, *Ancestors and Relatives: Genealogy, Identity, and Community* (New York: Oxford University Press, 2012), 131.

16. "Graduate Students' Perceptions of Their Advisors: Is There Systematic Disadvantage in Mentorship?," *Journal of Higher Education*, 83, 6 (November/December 2012): 879.

17. Chris M. Golde and George E. Walker, eds., *Envisioning the Future of Doctoral Education: Preparing Stewards of the Discipline* (San Francisco: Jossey-Bass, 2006).

18. In Chapter 2, p. 52.

19. Chris M. Golde, "Preparing Stewards of the Discipline," in Golde and Walker, eds., *Envisioning the Future*, 5.

20. Thomas Bender, Phillip F. Katz, and Colin A. Palmer, *The Education of Historians for the Twenty-First Century* (Urbana, IL: University of Illinois Press, 2004), 49.

21. David Damrosch, "Vectors of Change," in Golde and Walker, eds., *Envisioning the Future*, 38.

22. Ibid., 39.

23. Introduction, p. 3.

24. Stefan Collini, *What Are Universities For?* (London: Penguin, 2012), 8–9.

25. Michel Foucault, "What is an Author?," *Language, Counter-Memory, Practice: Selected Essays and Interviews*, ed. Donald F. Bouchard (Ithaca, NY: Cornell University Press, 1977), 131.

26. Ibid., 131.

27. Ibid., 131.

28. Ibid., 132.

29. Ibid., 132.

30. Ibid., 132.

31. Ibid., 134.

32. Thomas S. Kuhn, *The Structure of Scientific Revolutions*, 4th edn (Chicago: University of Chicago Press, 2012), 118.

33. Alex Haley, *Roots: The Saga of an American Family* (New York: Vanguard Books, 2007), 79.

34. http://www.rootsweb.ancestry.com/~websites/surnames/r.html, accessed May 17, 2017.

35. Walter Benjamin, "The Work of Art in the Age of Mechanical Reproduction," in *Illuminations*, tr. Harry Zohn, ed. Hannah Arendt (New York: Schocken Books, 1968), 220.

36. https://www.theguardian.com/uk-news/2015/mar/25/benedict-cumber-batch-is-related-to-richard-iii-scientists-say, accessed May 17, 2017.

37. Steven Pinker, "Strangled by Roots," *New Republic*, August 6, 2007, 32–3.

38. Haley, *Roots*, Acknowledgments.

39. http://freepages.genealogy.rootsweb.ancestry.com/~jbkeene/KeenePhillips/INDEX.HTML, accessed May 17, 2017.

40. Sigmund Freud, "Family Romances," in *The Standard Edition of the Complete Psychological Works of Sigmund Freud*, vol. IX (1906–8): "Jensen's 'Gradiva' and Other Works" (London: Hogarth Press, 1959), 235–42.

41. Henry Louis Gates, Jr, *Finding Your Roots* (Chapel Hill, NC: University of North Carolina Press, 2014), 16.

42. https://www.nytimes.com/2015/06/26/business/media/a-pbs-show-a-frustrated-ben-affleck-and-a-loss-of-face.html?_r=0, accessed June 4, 2017.

43. Gates, Jr, *Finding Your Roots*, 12.

44. http://www.pbs.org/wnet/aalives/2006/science_dna2.html, accessed May 17, 2017.

45. Zerubavel, *Ancestors and Relatives*, 131.

46. Julia Watson, "Ordering the Family: Genealogy as Autobiographical Pedigree," in *Getting a Life: Everyday Uses of Autobiography* (Minneapolis, MN: University of Minnesota Press, 1996), 300.

47. Catherine Nash, " 'They're Family!': Cultural Genealogies of Relatedness in Popular Genealogy" in Sara Ahmed, ed., *Uprootings/Regroundings: Questions of Home and Migration* (New York, Oxford: Berg Publishers, 2003), 180.

48. Graeme Davison, "Ancestors: The Broken Lineage of Family History," in *The Use and Abuse of Australian History* (St. Leonard's: Allen & Unwin, 2000), 81.

49. Ibid., 84.

50. Tanya Evans, "Secrets and Lies: the Radical Potential of Family History," *History Workshop Journal*, 71, 1 (2011): 49.

51. Ibid., 51.

52. Ibid., 52.

53. Graeme Davison, *Lost Relations: Fortunes of My Family in Australia's Golden Age* (Sydney: Allen & Unwin, 2015), xii.

54. Ibid., xiii.

55. Ibid., xiii.

56. Evans, "Secrets and Lies," 68.

57. Ibid., 57.

58. Davison, *Lost Relations*, xii.

59. Quoted in Séverine Louvel and Amy Jacobs, "Effects of Interdisciplinarity on Disciplines: A Study of Nanomedicine in France and California," *Revue française de sociologie* (English Edition), 56, 1 (2015): 64.

60. www.emory.edu, accessed May 17, 2017.

61. https://oakland.edu/Assets/upload/docs/AIS/Syllabi/Connor_Syllabus.pdf, accessed May 17, 2017.

62. Veronica Boix Mansilla, "Assessing Expert Interdisciplinary Work at the Frontier: An Empirical Exploration," *Research Evaluation*, 15, 1 (April 2006): 21.

63. Quoted in Gregorio Robles and Jesús M. González-Barahona, "A Comprehensive Study of Software Forks: Dates, Reasons and Outcomes," in Imed Hammouda, Björn Lundell, Tommi Mikkonen, and Walt Scacchi, (eds), *Open Source Systems: Long-Term Sustainability. OSS 2012. IFIP Advances in Information and Communication Technology*, vol. 378. (Berlin and Heidelberg: Springer, 2012): 1–13.

64. http://larrysanger.org/2004/12/why-wikipedia-must-jettison-its-anti-elitism/, accessed May 17, 2017.

65. https://www.gnu.org/philosophy/free-sw.en.html, accessed May 17, 2017.

5

Places to Think In

Library, Museum, Seminar

Until virtual, they're real, the universities: extended in space, dense with architecture, strewn with faculty, students, and staff, wired and networked, under (re)construction, never fully finished. People move with scheduled purposes. But think again how, alongside those purposefully and habitually on campus, you find visitors of many kinds: parents and siblings and applicants, delivery vans, taxis, the police. Pigeons and other fowl straggle on pavements. As I write, some students somewhere are in lecture or seminar, or in the library. Faculty are leading class or preparing for one, or at home, reading and writing. Between times, eating, greeting, and teasing occur. While some gaze through windows and think, others sweep and cook. Because the young are ascendant, high spirits give the dominant tone. But laughter is leavened with anxiety (said to have largely displaced depression), alongside resentment, arrogance, and uncertainty. In a culture of perpetual assessment and self-assessment, moods swing in many directions. If these are temples of learning, they are also multiform ecologies. I have argued for the abiding importance of solitary thought, but I take its value as no higher than that achieved through ongoing exchange. The university is a real and symbolic container of the negotiations between self and sociality. The present chapter attempts to think freshly about these conditions of community, both within and without the university.

Not yet virtual, academic spaces have grown more intricate and ambitious. By the turn of the new millennium, certainly by the end of its first decade, many universities were remaking their campuses and their self-understanding. Landscape and topography have changed.

Moreover, they've changed in ways that illuminate more than the physical dimension. The opening turn here is toward the recent architectural life of the university, as a worthy subject in itself and as an index of present conditions.

People in Buildings: New Campus Architecture and Mass Education

The university building boom of the last few years has appeared in different parts of the world under diverse administrative regimes with varying aims and urgencies. But the buildings themselves obey a striking similarity. They constitute, in effect, a new International Style of university architecture. Repeatedly, and almost definitionally, the style offers "postmodern" exteriors. The broken facades are often rich in color, with theatrical shapes and lightning; they use a mix of contemporary materials and often achieve a scale far greater than older buildings near them. Yet the surfaces of these new buildings give little indication of their educational purposes. They exist as flamboyant gestures creating sensations in their own right. From the standpoint of academic routine, the facades are inessential to the work of professors or their students—in a strict sense excessive. Many of the buildings recall the still resonating words of Robert Venturi, Denise Scott Brown, and Steven Izenour, who urged architects toward the postmodern pleasures of the "decorated shed."[1] Colorful surfaces can reach toward the splash of ornament with no reference to what they contain. The facades are masks that the building wears.

The worldwide turn to academic architectural postmodernity is an event of the new millennium, when these buildings began to appear in large number and at massive scale. They stand as marks of the contemporary that brand a university as up to date—physical signs of the present-becoming-future, signatures of the new. Within just the last decade, celebrity architects have brought their spectacle-achieving work to university grounds in many countries: Rem Koolhaas at Cornell, Frank Gehry at the University of Technology in Sydney, Zaha Hadid at the American University in Beirut, Norman Foster in Malaysia, Tadao Ando in Mexico. Four years ago, the *Financial Times* reflected on this new global manifestation, the "trophy buildings" that universities use "to reassert themselves or to update their image."[2]

Administrators frankly acknowledge that these gleaming structures—eye-catching, playful, contemporary—are instruments for soliciting student interest. They are signs of confidence and prestige, central to the competition for the best students and their tuition revenue.

But if we look beneath the postmodern surface, we find something arresting, yet familiar. Within the buildings appear the contours of a (slightly) older style, architectural modernism, an aesthetic favoring clean vectors, displaying objects in coherent space and providing sharp outlines, good light, simple colors. The interiors offer an incarnation of Louis Sullivan's dictum: *form* that proudly conforms to *function*, even as the facades ostentatiously separate the two. Adapting the words of Le Corbusier, we might say that the interiors are machines for learning in. On the emerging new campus, individual structures make a bid for uniqueness, laying claim to landmark status. Doing so, they implicitly suggest differentiation and heterogeneity among universities and within academic life; they mask the homogeneity of the standard-issue modernist task: the education of students on an industrial scale.

Beneath the splash effect of already famous buildings lives the real urgency, namely to accommodate the increasing number of students whom the university must now expect to receive. It must house them in the mass, teach them efficiently, and then award them duly with credentials and degrees and diplomas. Whatever the facades might win for reputation, the underlying demand is to design spaces adequate to the mass conditions of universities, at a time when the question is not whether education will occur in the mass, but how great a mass there will be. How many students can we educate? How many *should* we educate? How quickly? How well?

Then, even as we acknowledge the massification of higher education, we should notice something else about the design: namely its softness and relative comfort. The light, the seats, the sight lines, the acoustics are designed to meet the needs of individuals—one individual at a time. The lecture halls are spacious, some vast, but each chair in a hall is designed to contain the body of one student comfortably, one who has competed to earn a place on campus. A familiar local story tells of the student who finds the same seat every day and comes to regard it as his or her own. The new lecture hall is both a scene of contemporary massification and training, but also of a symbolically preserved individualism mirrored in the singular physical surfaces—a scene of collectivities and individuals.

In the publicity photographs favored by admissions' offices, students are rarely depicted in large groups, rather almost always in small units of two or three, and they often appear alone. Ample space is preserved between them to avoid suggestions of crowding. This too is an index of the topography. Hundreds and thousands of students occupy the grounds of a university, but they try to arrange themselves in small-scale groups, both physically and emotionally. Even small institutions threaten to overwhelm individuality. At bottom, the threat is a simple matter of physical/social circumstance: a (usually) young person encounters a large cohort of closely comparable others and must take steps to retain personhood ("I prefer my bed under the window"; "I refuse to start reading before I've had three cups of coffee").

Students often speak of their years before university, the years with their parents, as a phase of life that already seems distant and strange. To a degree that parents can be slow to understand, their children place themselves on the other side of a chasm. Like the postmodern buildings, every arriving student is an emblem of novelty. That past life is no longer this new one. At the same time, many (most) students frankly describe their years beyond graduation, the life to come, as radically unknown, even when their intentions are clear, and their will is strong. When asked how far into the future they imagine themselves, they typically reach only two or three years into post-university careers. Beyond that stretch only the possible outlines of a possible life. They may identify the employment they hope to hold—legal, medical, commercial—but in ways that they themselves emphasize, their descriptions are thin and unsure. They don't know where they will be, or with whom, or how it will come to pass.

Suspended between the world of their parents and a future seen faintly ahead, students have a disappearing past and an unknown future. What remains is an island of the present tense, often identified by year in university: "I'm a third year"; "I'm second"—their cohort being one of the first things students ask of one another. The university years become a self-conscious bracketing of time, or rather a temporality of their own, an island chapter in a life. "Making the most of these years" is one motto; "enjoying the freedom that will never come again" is another.

The chatting app Yik Yak, which allows anonymous conversation within a five-mile range, began in 2013; as it became pervasive, it was quickly turned to abusive, often racist purposes. After some high-profile cases, the developers took steps to limit access to "people college-aged and above." Whatever else it is or becomes, it stands as a window onto the wildly dispersed interests and quickly shifting rhetoric of undergraduates. The sex and toilet teasing is endless. But so are the loneliness, wistfulness, and wit:

> "I'm against nature. I don't dig nature at all. I think nature is very unnatural. I think the truly natural things are dreams, which nature can't touch with decay."
>
> "I can't be the only one waiting for student loan as a source of income and living on parents while job hunting am I?"
>
> "When you talk to someone every day and then one day they don't message."

It's familiar campus gassing, but then it's important not to overlook its place in the practice of undergraduate life. What Yik Yak makes visible is the pervasive low-level fret of self-fashioning: the abrupt swings in mood, the jokey self-deprecation, the irony–sincerity amalgam, the posing while listening to one's own voice. Part of what's striking is the movement between unfocused rumination on life's jagged pathways and the encounter with numerically precise assessment. Students suddenly externalize and objectify the agitations of their inner worlds. The materials for objectification are ready to hand: the need for a loan, the marks on an essay, the résumé or the CV which students compile as the exterior form of selfhood.

Simultaneously, of course, and more consequentially, the university is preparing its own indelible marks of value, worth, and distinction. Students flutter, sometimes complain, but finally have no choice but to accept numbers that become identity signs, permanently kept in the records office and sent on request to prospective employers. On any North American campus, students know their grade point averages down to at least two decimal points. The project of self-fashioning, forever thrust upon the late adolescent student, unfolds within these constraints; there are self-making individuals, and there is a university apparatus for sorting and branding graduates. Poignant messages on Yik Yak describe the collision between long-held plans and graded reality. Students come to feel newly defined, and then henceforth define themselves, through metrics they have been trained to accept but do not always understand.

From the standpoint of the faculty, the same population under the same constraints has a different aspect. When university instructors of any rank speak together, we frequently speak—do we not?—of "my course" or "my seminar." Or we refer to "my students." It's a feature of the work to create these possessive wholes and collectives. We ask one another, "How is the lecture going?" Even where the staff offers lectures or seminars together, the habit of the humanities is to disaggregate responsibilities. Accordingly, much of the work of teaching, like the research, is performed in closed rooms unseen by colleagues. The temptation is strong to personalize the experience, to dwell with justifiable pleasure on successes that seem to belong to *my* style and *my* rapport with *my* students.

To teach through time is to meet a succession of students, some remembered, many forgotten, so that we speak instinctively of generations: recent students—or students five years ago, or students nowadays, or when we were students. These groupings are prominent in the self-representation of university teachers. Yet we recognize these wholes as complex and unstable. The faculty know well that any seminar, any generation, can, and should, resolve into different persons, with separate histories, characters, and life trajectories. We mean to hold fast to individual personhood, as indeed we do with favorite and cherished students, and also with difficult and provocative ones. The exacting truth of the university world remains: we know and remember individuals, but we manage populations.

In the Library: Alone Together

Outside the walled garden it is different, quite different, but in important respects, the same. Take two other spaces where individuals move with others in acts of—or resembling—academic activity. The public library, to take its case first and briefly, is a well-used vessel of the everyday humanities. That it is free, that it requires minimal credential, that its materials can be handled without close supervision—these opportunities shouldn't be concealed by familiarity. Simply conjure the scene. An open volume of space (feeling large even in small libraries) allows room for singular curiosities. In many respects, the library—at, or out of, the university—is the space that most fully enables an individualism of the humanities. In front of a stack of books, a person of almost any age can give way to the power of silent absorption. Either leaning back to read more comfortably or bending forward to take notes on paper or screen, the library posture suggests a body adjusting to the demands of private concentration.

Most modern libraries still hew to the precedent of large high-ceilinged spaces. The continuing tradition means that even those deeply focused on their own books in their own space will be conscious of, and be in the consciousness of, all the others. It requires only a small exercise of defamiliarization to step back from the scene, which I inhabit as I write this sentence, in order to feel its awkwardness and interest. Two are elbows deep in today's newspaper; one hasn't moved in an hour; another taps her foot, and another licks his finger when he turns a page; the deputy librarian has a swivel chair that seems to swivel constantly. Seen from above, we must look like frozen mementos. The small noises of concentration—turning pages, scratching pencils, tapping keys—dissipate within the muffled silence. Even when groups of schoolchildren visit with teachers and volunteer parents, the norm of near-silence respects the furrowed brows that ignore one another in this community of isolates.

Eccentricity still flourishes in public libraries, eccentricity of interest and manner. Muttering, sighing, shabby clothes, and eye contact can worry parents and annoy the staff, but in the absence of real disruption, eccentricity can usually make its way. Partly, this is because even the most sanctioned conduct—quiet sustained reading—can take on the look, and virtue, of the eccentric. Let them all be. Which indeed is what many librarians contentedly do. The difficulty, if it is a difficulty, is that the generous dispersal of individualities in the library has so little social motion. Friendships, one supposes, can accidentally be made. Certainly, individual achievements are frequent: stories are read; letters, and books, get written; browsing and ruminating and deliberating and resolving are done. But a common experience is rarely achieved, not on a given day, not over a series of months. The staff is generally in short supply and harried by everyday responsibilities. Even when events are on offer, reading groups or conversations, the public library is dominated by the separateness of its visitors. Any late morning visit on a weekday will be both an exhibit of human loneliness and the dignity of autonomy.

What Do the Museums Want from Us?

How far otherwise is it with museums, which make a more difficult case? Although the library at any university is more prominent and heavily used than any museum it may fortunately have, it's the latter that shares more with, and differs more interestingly from, academic life. At any large museum, the curatorial staff approaches the scale of small university departments. Advanced degrees are common, while the records of publication can be as distinguished as that of any other scholar. A teaching mission guides and inspires much of the work. Many events—lectures, symposia—are indistinguishable from academic offerings. Movement is frequent between museums and departments of art history and archaeology.

A difference, surely the largest, is the relation with the public that arrives to be edified and instructed. Its membership is inconstant, even for those who are "members." No degrees, of course, and no curriculum. As an institution in its own right and a space to itself, the museum keeps apart from the logic of academic progress. School groups, it's true, gather on the floor before a painting; university courses put collections to serious use. There are individual lectures; short courses are sometimes offered. But the everyday life of a museum depends on the unplanned visit of uninstructed individuals, who are neither required to turn up nor obliged to learn.

From the moment in the eighteenth century when exhibitions moved out of controlled, usually private spaces (cabinets of curiosity) into a public realm, the audience became an anxiety. Who would they be? How many? And how would they comport themselves? The opening of the British Museum was at the same time a courting of the risk of the unknown public. The nervousness reached crescendo in the middle of the next century during the Great Exhibition of 1851, a temporary museum that marks a crossing point in the history of public display. The physical scale (inside the immense Crystal Palace in Hyde Park), the unbroken attention of newspapers and journals, the global reach of the artifacts, and the self-conscious modernity in both the bureaucratic organization and the style of display—these created the legendary aura of the event, well before it opened. The question mark concerned the audience. It was taken for granted that a rapt crowd would gather; indeed it did. "Never," wrote Henry Mayhew, "was there was such a crowd congregated in any part of London, and certainly in no other part of the world. The multitudes that had entered the Building were but as a few grains of sand collected, as it were, from the vast shore of human beings without."[3]

They would swarm through the aisles; this was taken for granted. But would they behave? In particular, would the working classes behave? Anxiously anticipated, the affordable Shilling Days approached. Warnings came from the police. Advice descended upon the workers. When the first Shilling Day passed in reassuring calm, a sigh of social peace was exhaled, and the nimbus of success was preserved. Yet already a structure of expectation had formed. On one side, ambitious display required extensive forethought, arrangement, and supervision; on the other side, appropriate viewing demanded attention and obedience. The groups—curators/administrators and the public—belonged to different realms. Their relation was uneasy.

A few years after the Great Exhibition, Dickens wrote a short, teasing account of his visit to the Palace at Hampton Court to view the famous works of art. Under the title "Please to Leave Your Umbrella," the essay evokes the charged moment of entry into the protected space of display. Dickens meets a police guard who makes the titled request; he complies, but then mulls over his willing compliance. What does it mean to be so obedient to the canons of conduct? What else is relinquished with his umbrella?

> Please to put into your umbrella, to be deposited in the hall until you come out again, all your powers of comparison, all your experience, all your individual opinions. Please to accept with this ticket for your umbrella the individual opinions of some other personage whose name is Somebody, or Nobody, or Anybody, and to swallow the same without a word of demur. Be so good as to leave your eyes with your umbrellas, gentlemen, and to deliver up your private judgment with your walking-sticks.[4]

You surrender judgment with the umbrella, and then still more. Your personal temperament and character must also be suspended: "Leave your umbrella and take up your gentility. Taste proclaims to you what is the genteel thing; receive it and be genteel!...Think no more for yourselves—be you the care of the Police of Taste!"[5] It's an early moment in the history of museum culture, but already a central agitation shows itself. Those responsible for the collection lay out the terms of encounter. The visitors understand they must accept rules of behavior. In two centuries of modern museumship, consider how many children have been told, "Don't touch the objects. Don't even get too close." Always an attendant is nearby. You move through rooms with a consciousness of small serious surveillance.

Intermittently, but inevitably, we also watch one another. As Dickens begins his stroll past the paintings, he notices "one other visitor (in very melancholy boots): who soon went his long grave way, alternately dark in the piers and light in the windows, and was seen no more."[6] An encounter is averted. But the mention reminds us that a regular element of museum visiting lies with the accident of strangers who happen to be visiting then too. By chances of the clock or digestion or whim, we find ourselves alongside unknown others, making an accidental society. Whether we come alone or with company, the assumption is that we will leave the strangers to themselves and their own rhythms of attention.

The force of Hardy's poem "In the British Museum" is to confuse that assumption and to raise the stakes of encounter. Part of the subtle excitement of every visit, after all, is the chance to break the cocoon around separate selves and acknowledge that even if we share nothing else, we're both standing before that startling piece of something. As Hardy's poem begins, a visitor steps forward and addresses another:

> "What do you see in that time-touched stone,
> When nothing is there
> But ashen blankness, although you give it
> A rigid stare?
>
> "You look not quite as if you saw,
> But as if you heard,
> Parting your lips, and treading softly
> As mouse or bird.
>
> "It is only the base of a pillar, they'll tell you,
> That came to us
> From a far old hill men used to name
> Areopagus."[7]

This is a voice of initiation, stylized in its certainty. Some move more easily than others inside the museum; some are familiar with the ways of viewing; some know (or believe they know) what there is to be seen. ~~Hardy begins with the asymmetry. This voice of questioning is also a~~ voice of chastening: the stone is "only the base of a pillar": "nothing is there." But the words returned are startling in their defiance:

> "I know no art, and I only view
> A stone from a wall,
> But I am thinking that stone has echoed
> The voice of Paul,
>
> "Paul as he stood and preached beside it
> Facing the crowd,
> A small gaunt figure with wasted features,
> Calling out loud
>
> "Words that in all their intimate accents
> Pattered upon
> That marble front, and were far reflected,
> And then were gone.
>
> "I'm a labouring man, and know but little,
> Or nothing at all;
> But I can't help thinking that stone once echoed
> The voice of Paul."

These seven stanzas give the poem, and also give a parable of the museum in modernity. The sophisticated first voice is silenced by the strong second utterance. Here is someone whose vision is not to be tutored. The "labouring man" will openly confess deficiency according to the standards of display (I "know no art" and "know but little"). But nothing, including the exercise of his will, can stop the course of thoughts: "I can't help thinking."

A third presence hovers over the scene, showing itself in the first speaker's remark that "It is only the base of a pillar, they'll tell you." The unnecessary-to-specify "they" is the collective authoritative voice. It has already trained the first speaker, who promptly transmits its expertise. By the end of the nineteenth century, as Simon Knell has noted, archaeology had matured as a discipline and had assumed a leading, often dominant role in the curating community.[8] Certainly within Hardy's poem, archaeology sets the terms and limits of knowledge. It specifies the object ("base of a pillar") and its provenance ("Areopagus"). It takes away even as it gives: "It is only the base of a pillar." Dickens had resisted the policing in taste. Just a few decades later, Hardy records the quiet ascendancy of a regime of knowledge.

The force of the final stanzas lies in their exposure of authority's limits. The laborer concedes the rights of empiricism within its domain ("I only view / A stone from a wall"), but holds to the rights of non-empirical reverie, the claim of a "thinking" that offers more vivid images and richer narrative. This dimension of the contrast should be well marked. "They" have conducted the secular project of modern museumship, founded on material evidence leading to ascertainable truth. It's telling that from the standpoint of the authorities at the British Museum the stone belongs to the "pagan" world of ancient Greece, identified only as from the Areopagus (the hill of Ares, northwest of the Acropolis where the senior court of Athens met). "They" make no mention of Paul, who in Acts 17 preaches his sermon of faith to the Greeks assembled on the hill. But Hardy's "labouring man", though he humbly admits to knowing "nothing at all," asserts that he can see Paul and evoke him (the "small gaunt figure with wasted features").

In central respects, Hardy's visitor has lost the struggle that began in the nineteenth century. Within the secular culture of the world's dominant museums, religion is a practice like any other. Sacred articles are handled with care, not as incitements to faith or emotional transport, but as objects of ethnographic interest, duly labeled and contextualized. The British Museum stands as an epitome of arch-aeological equanimity: no matter what religious ecstasy may have once attended the artifact, it is restored to its place in a secular story. In many of the world's capitals, museums have become the alternative to church, even as self-conscious rivals on any given Sunday. The visitors at a museum must stand and circulate. Opportunities are rare for gestures of devotion, for kneeling and praying.

In the hundred thirty years since Hardy's poem, the academic ambitions of museums have grown. As the movement of ideas (and people) between museum and university quickens, the presence of "They" has consolidated. Most visitors place themselves comfortably in the hands of the staff, preparing to be enlarged, edified, educated. They join the spirit of seriousness, move along the indicated path. On the other side, directors and curators strive for the rigorous application of expert authority. In an essay of the middle nineties, Neil MacGregor, then director of the National Gallery in London, quoted the Annual Report of the Trustees. The report celebrated the success of major exhibits, which has relied on scrupulous research; in the coolly confident words of the document:

> The exhibits demonstrated incontrovertibly that scholarship and public access are not, as has sometimes been asserted, alternatives between which museums and galleries must choose. Rather it is scholarship which adds a new dimension to accessibility. In consequence, we believe it is essential that scholarship remain a priority if we are to serve the ever larger public we expect in the next few years.[9]

MacGregor embraces the "trickle-down effect of scholarship," which has become "very, very fast and very, very effective."[10] Accordingly, the gallery has hired more curators.

The subtle argument of the suave essay is that "scholarship" is essential to the museum, but that it must serve the "public." It cannot be research for its own sake. This is the insistent point: "Our purpose in our scholarship must be better to conserve our collections and, above all, better to allow the public to enjoy and to understand." The rhetoric evokes an equilibrium between curator and audience. Visitors arrive with a thirst for knowledge. It can be quenched. As long as scholarship remembers its audience, then a contract of exchange will be preserved. The expert will provide the gift of understanding to the lay mind. That gift will be ratified through presentations, where, for instance, curators explain "why they hang [a picture] in a particular way."[11]

That MacGregor has identified a genuine social/cultural condition is a point validated by his personal success as well as the success of the museums he has directed. It's also telling, if familiar, that his word for the hundreds of thousands of visitors is "the public." From the perspective of governments as well as trustees, each who enters the space is a countable particular. The essay exults in the numbers: "160,000" people attended the exhibition "Art in the Making."[12] Yet we know that one of the marked changes of the last generation has been the differentiation of audiences. The demand by policymakers for wider "access" has grown total numbers but also, and by design, has increased heterogeneity: MacGregor's 160,000 are not interchangeable.

Nor have they ever been—as Hardy's laborer "In the British Museum" stubbornly shows. He suggests something else. In the simple assertion of what he "thinks," he asserts a refusal of consensus, of curator-think. And then it's also worth reflecting that no matter what he sees or believes, whether too heterodox or orthodox, he is unlikely to be asked to leave. The authorities protect the objects, but for all of Dickens's worry, they are unable to police stray thought. This is the hushed continuous drama around the pedestals and display cases. The space of the museum can determine the display of information, can dictate the routes of movement, can stipulate restrictions and, if necessary, acts of discipline. The disposition of uniform-wearing guards and attendants can be formidable. Also, the accidental community in any given room exerts a pressure. If you keep blocking the gaze of those behind you, a mutter or an "excuse me" might urge you along. Visitors feel these constraints, but like Hardy's guest at the British Museum, they may have thoughts that they "can't help thinking."

A room in a museum is a volume of space, supervised but still open enough for wandering movement, physical and psychological. Within wide enough limits, the space permits an independent absorption. You can gaze, as Hardy's laborer gazes, with a "rigid stare" and parted lips. You can speak (softly, if you're good) to the person alongside you. Even in small museums, the space must be disposed to allow physical motion. From time to time, visitors may disrupt the area: mocking, complaining, moving too fast, flaunting lack of interest. Someone might sneer, "That's not art," or simply, "It's too crowded." More common, though more elusive, are the acts of private silent refusal—a withdrawal of attention or a reluctant sinking into boredom.

What, after all, do the curators want for us, and from us? MacGregor at the National Gallery is, in one respect, staunch and clear:

> I believe our job in the National Gallery—and the function of scholarship in the National Gallery—is to enable the public to move around the past with confidence. They need the confidence that there are fixed points, individual objects which have been identified, dated, established, and various routes around those fixed points which they can follow and from which, if they like, pursue others.[13]

The image is crystalline. The past is singular; it comes in a diagram connecting the deposits of history ("fixed points"), which are open to public view, but only once they have been well "established" by the scholar/curator. But the carefully arranged image, like something that could hang in the gallery, struggles to keep its fragile balance. Without scholarship, no fixity, no routes, no dating, identifying, or establishing. Yet, once the scholars have laid the past open to view, then the striding public will be "enabled." Confidence will mark its movements. And as MacGregor works through the logic of the exchange, he lets the balance tilt to the side of the now-illuminated visitor:

> ultimately the exploration, the taking possession, has to be a personal one. There can be no doubt that we have to move on our own through the collections. We have ultimately to make our own decisions. I think that the role, then, of the scholars or the curators is not to put themselves between the public and the objects, not in any very elaborate sense to explain the objects, but to exhort the visitor to a direct experience, to an unmediated vision.[14]

Two "ultimately"s and this suddenly inviting "we." MacGregor himself rejoins the public: he too belongs to "we" who have the right to take possession of the objects, to make their meanings "personal" as the effects of our own "decisions." The rigorous labors of scholarship liberate each of us to our direct private experience.

Captions Or Objects: Learning Or Seeing

The oscillating emphasis lays bare the deep double-sidedness of museum culture. It stands at a nexus where the academic and everyday humanities come close, socially and spatially. Often on site but usually out of view, technical subjects are rigorously pursued. The science of conservation remains in the hands of trained practitioners. Designers adjust the light and the walls for hanging. Curators delve into their research, frequently calling on scholars based in the university. In the case of a large exhibit, a handsome catalogue may be the outcome, the work of professors alongside curators, available in libraries and in the museum's gift shop. But even close collaborators from universities typically connect to the museum only for the length of a given project. The staff of the museum itself—director, curators, designers, conservators—remains a relatively closed domain, its norms and standards developed through professional consensus, seeing one another day by day, while the others come and go.

Yet the central justification for a museum, and the basis for most philanthropy and government provision, remains exhibition. Even as the professional tasks become more specialized, the demand for wider access increases. Curatorial professionalism and public access mark the site where the institutional "contradiction" is most pointed. MacGregor writes of the need to prepare the visitor, to identify, date, and establish, the routes between those fixed points disclosed by scholarship. All this careful work is said to be in preparation for direct experience, personal decisions, and "unmediated vision." Unmediated? In what sense? The experience, we are told, depends on the sedulous labor of scholarship. What are all those routes and points if not deeply thought, carefully prepared mediations?

The subject attracts keen debate nowadays. A strong and recurrent position is that visitors should be set free to encounter objects beyond the framework of scholarship. Sandra H. Dudley has cast the problem as a neglect of objects themselves in favor of the critical aims of the curators:

> Objects matter within museum practice, of course—but where some of them at least would have been used to awe and inspire visitors, today they more often feature as, effectively, grammatical marks punctuating a story being told, rather than as powerful items in their own right. The effort expended by museums to render objects and interpretation accessible, and to enable visitors to identify meaning and context, is laudable and important; yet arguably it may sometimes be the strategies employed in that very effort which prevent or limit the opportunities for directly encountering and responding to objects in and of themselves, prior or in addition to cognitively exploring the stories they have to tell. The challenge lies in producing successful and accessible interpretive interventions which simultaneously do not act to dilute, if not remove altogether, the sense of magic, mystery and excitement that objects can also convey.[15]

Where Neil MacGregor finds reassuring convergence of research and experience, Dudley belongs to a recent group of skeptics. She cites, as do others, the suggestions of James Clifford that we restore to objects "their lost status as fetishes. Our fetishes. This tactic, necessarily personal, would accord to things in collections the power to fixate, rather than simply the capacity to edify or inform."[16] According to Ernst van de Wetering:

> The increasingly sophisticated facilities, ingenious showcases and theatrical lighting in museums are leading to the taming and stylization of the often somewhat unintentionally savage air that clings to many objects, hinting at past calamities. Many restoration and conservation treatments have, often unintentionally, a subtle cosmetic effect that leaves the objects imperceptibly well groomed, so that they comply with museum style.[17]

The puzzle is there for all to see. Objects come draped with nearby captions, handy brochures, and information boards. A highly trained eye will proudly turn directly to the object. But for the everyday visitor, including the specialist who happens to concentrate upon a different period, there remains the nervousness of ignorance. You tell yourself to look first at the object, to give yourself to perception and sensation. But then you find yourself sinking into the old dependency. The pivot of attention creates the consciousness of bad faith. Have we failed the object? Have we failed ourselves?

The demand takes diverse forms, from Clifford's "fetishes" and Julie Marcus's "erotics of the museum" to Dudley's more moderate plea for museums to "ponder what it would be like for visitors more often than not to be able properly, bodily, emotionally to engage with an object rather than look at it half-heartedly prior to, or even after, reading a text panel on a wall or a label in a case."[18] These are calls to restore what Benjamin described as the "authority of the object"[19] that he sees waning in the age of mechanical reproduction. It also wanes under the weight of information. Dudley describes her accidental encounter with a Chinese horse displayed in a small museum, unencumbered by label or explanation.[20] The shattering immediacy of the experience is what she misses in the contemporary museum. Adam Bencard has been part of a group agitating for the display of the human remains held in Medical Museion in Copenhagen. The pieces range "from spines malformed by tuberculosis to skulls dissolved by syphilis and skeletons of anencephalic newborns."[21] Bencard explains that the point of the exhibition is not for its scientific value or for the stories that might usefully be drawn from the objects. The project is in search of "presence."[22] It asks viewers to ask "what happens when you actually see it," drawing on Kathleen Stewart's call to "slow the quick jump to representational thinking and evaluative critique long enough to find ways of approaching the complex and uncertain objects that fascinate because they literally hit us or exert a pull on us."[23]

This active and continuing debate unsettles MacGregor's equilibrium of information and experience, research and wonder, science and presence. But the ambiguities can be seen as productive as well as agitating. The professionalization of the museum staff—the training, the differentiation of roles, the self-consciousness of aim and aspiration—stands adjacent, often quite near, to the amorphous public which knows itself as more contingent than coherent. On Tuesdays, there are school groups. Sundays are crowded. In July, tourists overrun the place. Unlike faculty and students, museum staff and public only rarely make a connection. They don't expect to take coffee together, or to lock brains in pursuing a knotty problem. Even when a symposium or gallery talk is thrown, a gap remains between the hosting curator and the shuffling audience. Unlike the classroom, the museum cannot expect that those who enter its spaces will attain some competence, if not excellence, in the subject, and that most who pass an hour will have reached a benchmark of understanding. It's not only that visitors make a diverse group; it's also that individuals come with a diversity of interests, including an interest in not anticipating too much from their visit.

This dissonance of aim between staff and visitors may be unfortunate, but it also gives an opening for surprise and improvisation. Even in the spirit of well-trained cooperation, uncertainty gathers. How long, for instance, should one stand in front of an artifact? No one can say. But the question looms for most museum-goers (you can tell). In the presence of a grand piece—especially one that is dramatically framed and lit—conscience harries the viewer. You feel you should look more deeply, concentrate more fully. You wonder about the reactions of others: Why are they all crowded around that piece? And wonder, too, about your own clarity of vision: Am I identifying what the caption describes? Will I remember what I'm seeing now? The humility of the museum-goer only grows with recognition that the display represents a mere abbreviation of broader unseen knowledge. The archeology or acquisition that brought an object here, and the research and interpretation lying behind the presentation: these are glimpsed as if from outside a sanctum. Understanding thins as it moves from specialist to curator to designer to the wall next to an object. To become familiar with the main styles of exhibition is to see the display as ellipsis, the surface manifestation that floats on deep learning. Do I even know what I've seen?

The visit can take the aspect, and meet the needs, of an academic encounter; it can be organized by topic, period, or artist, laid out toward articulate goals, and often topped off with a handsome publication, the catalogue. Yet, the absence of marking and grading is key. Museums may be cleverly integrated into school or university courses, but for the great mass of visitors, no metrics of performance (beyond self-monitoring) need ever disturb the gazing. There is no curriculum, no exam at the end of the afternoon. The demands on performance remain low, not much more than, "Don't touch." Even as visitors nurse their curiosity, they know themselves as immune to the stresses of appraisal and rank.

A mix of liberation and regulation pervades the viewing rooms, corridors, and foyers. The line between leisure and education loses clarity. Uneasiness shadows gain: the visitor moves through the rooms knowing that no one leaves with a fully stocked visual memory. Muted voices can manufacture solemnity, but also absurdity. An upsurge of resistance can suddenly appear, an insistence on the rights of relative judgment and idiosyncratic experience, the echo of Hardy's "labouring man." No one can keep the visitor from loss of interest, or disgust, or counter-narrative.

Private Hoards, Public Needs

A visit to a museum is most often an encounter with objects on the human scale: paintings or sculpture that one's own front entry could in principle accommodate, or ancient tools and implements that could fit, if necessary, into your pantry. For every whisper of longing, "If only that were mine!," there comes a different gasp, "I wouldn't hang that thing on my wall." But in either case, there's always a perception, both confusing and enticing, that the objects occupy a different order of being. They belong in some other realm. They are thinkably possessed, but permanently unreachable. The injunction "Don't touch" suggests more than bodily restraint. It's an assertion of rights and values that exceed the viewer.

Collections, however, also live at home. To return from the museum may not be to find barren and empty rooms; in a striking proportion of cases, the home (or garage, or loft, or basement) is the site of personal collection. Susan Pearce has observed that "In the Western world something around 30% of people ... now collect something. Whatever else collecting is, it is a major social phenomenon."[24] The range of objects can seem endless: stamps and coins, of course, but also sports memorabilia, mugs, miniature cars and trains, toy soldiers, beer bottles, spice jars, etc., etc., etc. The mere impulse to gather, arrange, consider, and exhibit (if only to friends and family) is neither mean nor insignificant. It stirs pride; it also generates sustained life projects. The personal collection can be extended, but also reconsidered. Although it rarely comes with informational placards posted alongside, it has its own concepts and context.

The spreading success of television's *Antiques Roadshow* is an unmistakable sign of interest. Far from the formality of a museum, an unswept attic contains wonders. Retrieved and dusted, an object may reveal not only its forgotten origin and secret history but also its surprising value. An owner displays the item proudly/shyly, contributes a short personal story and describes the curving course that led to this piece being here and now ("Well, I inherited it from my father, who used to collect antiques and curiosities").[25] The expert-interlocutor enjoys the tale ("It's a cracking story"), but speaks with the authority of (prepared) information, filling in backgrounds that no everyday owner could have known. This second narrative gives a different pleasure: the satisfaction of lifting a fragment (physical fragment) out of the density of private life and burnishing it with contexts and perspectives. The punchline arrives in good time: "Any idea what it's worth?" The figure is often gratifyingly high—so much for that dusty thing?—as the owner's head lifts in pleasing surprise, "Really?,," "Good heavens!," "Really!" The appraisal is the clinching denouement because on television an object is never not commodity. In easy homespun style, the show lays out a division between the value of knowledge ("The watermark shows 1798") and the seductions of profit. It may only be the hope that stirs this book, but my own viewings suggest that the energy of the telecast is all on the side of knowing, not selling.

Another dimension of collecting is found on eBay. Money, of course, is a motor here too. It can be difficult to piece through the big players and the splash ads. But with determined scrolling, and partly because of its origin, the site still allows taste to show itself with minimal interference. What's striking is the specification of interests. The world turns out to be full of people who not only collect *kinds* of things but can now aim for ever more defined particularities. Some sell, and others quickly buy, items such as "Small Koi Fish Design Lined Jewel Jewelry Box," "Collectible Golf Tees & Leather Pouch," and "Carved Cheeky CAT wooden Hair Pin BARRETTE Clip Clasp Slide Handmade Sono Wood." A ship-in-a-bottle ornament comes with this ornate but characteristic description:

> What a wonderful find! A RARE glass ship in a bottle, authentic, it is known as an "Age of Sail" ornament. It has an inner protective box enclosed in an outer box. Approx. 2 7/8 inches high with a corkstopper and red ribbon. It is glass and will be packed in bubble wrap. The detail on this is amazing, and it would make a wonderful gift for the sailor in your life, or just if you love unique, beautiful ornaments on your tree. Great stocking stuffer!

The new technology lets the quester search planetary holdings for rarities. Meticulous descriptions correspond to the precision of desires. But though they grow from singular temperaments and distant sources, the object-desires connect people in subcultures of ardent enthusiasm. The meeting of taste and interest can remain on the small or medium scale—from the display of new finds to friends and family to multi-day conventions on the scale of Comic-Con. Susan Pearce reminds us that for all the monetizing of private collections, most of the gathered objects are "junk"[26]—that is, possessed for free or close to nothing. But then it's worth remembering that in the higher reaches of privilege, collecting is perhaps the most expensive habit on the globe. Jewelry, furniture, and especially fine art create boom (and bust) times within the large auction houses and, important to purposes here, create an alternative subculture of expert opinion, careful presentation, and managed viewing.

These last issues have an increasingly important consequence. As budgets for museums and libraries teeter from one retrenchment to the next, new acquisitions are kept within narrow limits. Only a few museums in the world can routinely acquire the most desirable pieces. The effect is that vast numbers of precious objects move into private holding, leaving curators to negotiate for gifts or at least temporary exhibition. Museum narratives of artists and movements contain gaping holes, where important works have been removed from public view.

The second growing tendency comes from a quite different direction. This is the growing interest of museums in local and material culture. Not the cherished and canonized masterworks but the objects of everyday existence: domestic utensils, public signs, car fins, telephones, clothing, etc. Active scholars and curators share their widening interest with a public aroused to curiosity about the ordinary lived past. Here too the museum looks outside its walls and its holdings to keep its mission open and alive.

The Humanities and Religion: Rivals and Complements

These activities, in real and virtual space, extend outward from individual curiosity. Only in rare cases do we find jealous guarding, rather than proud exhibition, of the new poet discovered in a library or the antique jewelry acquired at the flea market or Sotheby's. But the social circles and Facebook groups formed around these enthusiasms are difficult to sustain. Because the task of collection is usually seen as appendage to the serious stem of life, its claims on attention tend to be muted, or when unmuted, annoying.

What universities possess, almost all of them, is a minimum durability that allows a community of knowledge to persist. The fizzing energies outside the academy should be seen, affirmed, engaged. The failure to do so glares: it's undemocratic and counter to the cause of inquiry. Seen from an outside perspective, the academic world has the resources (intellectual, social, monetary, institutional), the merest sliver of which would let the everyday humanities avoid the hazards of dispersal and discontinuity. For all the irritations of university bureaucracy, it keeps students and faculty on record and lets them know when to turn up. But more important than the bureaucratically constituted community are the acts of affiliation and membership that all remember but most are too shy to relate.

Terry Eagleton has been making the case for religion as the time-tested institution resisting the secular substitutions so many intellectuals have proposed. Can religion really be surpassed, asks Eagleton? Can its satisfactions and benefits be found elsewhere? When displaced—for instance, into sport—religion stubbornly reappears in new forms (a "canon of legendary heroes," a "sense of solidarity"). When attacked in one region of the world (the capitalist West), it flourishes in another (Islamic nations).

> It has, in fact, proved to be by far the most tenacious, enduring, widespread, deep-seated symbolic system humanity has ever known, not least because it is able to connect the everyday customs and practices of billions of ordinary people with the most august, transcendent, imperishable truths. It's the most *successful* form of popular culture in human history, though I wager you won't find it on a single cultural studies course.[27]

"Religion" of course contains multitudes: not only diverse faiths, but a profusion of activities, formal and informal, institutional and anti-institutional. Even conceding the point, though, we might ask whether the practice of religion is more enduring than the practice of education, which is just as profusely various, as abiding and widespread. Eagleton follows Charles Taylor in seeing "belief" as "constitutive of selfhood";[28] capitalism and atheistic intellectuals naively assume we can live without its anchor. But is achieved belief in Eagleton's sense more constitutive than the project of inquiry? Is settled conviction a more profound need than a curiosity to know?

Undecidable questions, but to pose them is at least to acknowledge the salient issue. *Pace* Eagleton, the religious life has never been alone as a persistent system of symbols, or indeed as inspiration calling to vocation. We know that during many centuries, church and university were so closely intersecting as to be one, and indeed as far back as we can see, the task of education, formal/informal, stands as a parallel symbolic activity. Secular education now stands largely, though not fully, apart from religious practice, but we can revive a question posed briefly in an earlier chapter: Why should universities come under scrutiny that churches escape? Or, put in present terms, why does formal belief have greater claim than openness to knowledge?

Especially in the UK, the government now thinks nothing of generating an immense apparatus of assessment in order to weigh the "excellence" of research and to allocate funds accordingly. Can one imagine the machinery of appraisal turned on the churches? How would one populate the panels? What metrics would be employed? Could standards of comparative international ranking also be applied to the various religions? Would interfaith relations stand in parallel to interdisciplinary research? And would "excellence" pertain to quality of sermon, tunefulness of choir, and reach of evangelism ("impact")?

Hands are kept almost entirely off the inner workings of religious faith and church practice; the rare interventions make for stories in the press. Hands off the university, then. It too is a time-tested domain of full-dimensioned human experience. If belief can be solemnly respected in the churches, let inquiry be allowed to follow its many paths on the campus. Naturally, there will be failure, even turpitude, in universities as in churches. But in the absence of glaring or systematic or widespread failure, why not defer to the preponderant virtue of those who pursue the calling? The faculty—trust them. Trust the faculty.

One other issue comes to the surface here. For many people, the humanities belong to, and are regularly found within, religious settings. These may be days of worship in temple, synagogue, church, or mosque when the service turns to matters that exceed the theological and ritual contexts. The sacred texts raise issues of linguistic, literary, philosophic, and historical importance and are often approached as such. Then, outside the formal service come all the associated gatherings and the special occasions where co-religionists meet and raise questions, among others, that are familiar in university precincts. Those who ponder the next turn in the humanities do well to keep the religious activities visible. Of all the extra-university opportunities, these are prevalent, long-tested and too little acknowledged. For those like me who call out for more humanities everywhere, we need to accept that many feel they get what they need by conducting lives of religious faith that, as Eagleton fairly claims, connect "everyday customs and practices" to "august, transcendent, imperishable truths."[29]

His argument, though, moves on a distortingly high plane of abstraction: "religion," as if the varieties are hardly worth acknowledging, and "transcendent, imperishable truths," as if the differences between them pose no challenge to their truthfulness. Where has Eagleton been in all of his university positions that he hasn't noticed the connection between the humanities and the pursuit of deep (though thankfully not "imperishable") truth? Of course, it's different, but then we want it to be different. No scripture founds academic research. Its task depends on resisting, by no means always successfully, the hardening of mobile thought into scriptural permanence.

Eagleton is right to talk about the depletion of selfhood, the loss of its many-sidedness, and also right to insist that many people, now as in the past, turn to religion to meet human needs otherwise unsatisfied. If I propose the humanities as worthy rival and complement to religion, I acknowledge its only intermittent sufficiency. In fair measure this is due to the narrowing paths of university careers, tightened around entrepreneurial career-building at every stage, and encumbered with CV-applicable benchmarks that invite the never-finished caressing of individual achievement.

The academic humanities live within the university, and the university belongs to the wider network of economic demand and political constraint. Still, much of the responsibility lies with those who perform the daily routines of department and disciplinary life. No one should doubt the attainments effected through the professionalization of the humanities. From systems of peer review to more rigorous standards of evidence; from the meritocratic weighting of research to the production of scrupulously edited journals; from the advocacy of professional societies to the better training of doctoral students; from commitments to diversity to ethical standards in teaching, hiring, and promoting—these represent historically imperative benchmarks.

Yet professionalization always risks becoming an engineering project, a set of protocols that pass from being usefully habitual to fixed and then automatic. It's not only external bodies that have imposed metrics of success upon the humanities. They have also been self-imposed. The number of published books and articles; the ranking of journals; award of prizes; and service on local, national, and international committees—these can be, and are, measured, compared, and evaluated as part of a professional profile. Fine and good.

Finer and better, though, if professionalism unfolds with consciousness of its costs. Anyone who practices the humanities, in or out of the university, knows that its values and contributions exceed the published productivity of faculty, the vita-burnishing of doctoral students, and the numerical marking of undergraduates. Phrases like "intellectual passion," "sense of calling," "inspiration" are ever vulnerable to another effect of professionalism: its irony. But there should be less embarrassment, and more considered discussion, of the values—also social benefits, moral virtues—of the humanities that exceed and resist their professionalism. It's right to remember that the professional humanities are a recent phenomenon, no more likely to be permanent in their present state than at other phases in a long history. A better future will lie in asserting the many dimensions of their value, of which professionalism is both indispensable and increasingly distorted, largely but not only by forces beyond its reach.

It's useful, then, within a reflection on the spaces of community, to end with conversation across a table in the seminar room. The lecture hall retains a place in the humanities; I spend much of my own time there. But within the organization of curriculum, the memory of participants, and the structure of pedagogy, the seminar has privilege—though its satisfactions are not as self-evident as its difficulties. Sometimes the problem is the weak improvisation of a poorly prepared instructor, sometimes the sluggishness of tired students. Even when the level of contribution is high, misfires are abundant. The one who says too much is only slightly more disruptive than the several who say nothing at all. A characteristic aim of the seminar is to focus upon a problem or two—a text, image, or sound; an interpretation; a student paper; a philosophic argument; or a question of influence or context. The direction of exchange is kept open; this is the point: to weigh responses and to let them develop in reaction to one another. A risky procedure. With luck, digressions will make their way back to a common concern, and the array of contributions begin to have some shape. Still, no one expects a work of argumentative art to grow from on-the-spot thought. Invariably, there will be halting movement, repetition, incomprehension, annoyance. Students compete with one another and mock their professors. Many are the times when participants leave with few notes, if any.

Nevertheless, the seminar retains commitment and continues to stir conviction. It may mark the best validation of the humanities, where it most clearly stands as complement and rival to religion. Even its misfires are part of its power, the signs of thought struggling to comprehend itself. If the lower jealousies are on display, so are the better feelings of mere curiosity and the pleasure taken in shared pondering. The laughter during a sharp surprising turn can signal a small community coming into being. Although some students never overcome shyness or disdain, many test their voices in memorably satisfying ways. The strength to try a thought in public and the capacity to open another's thought to new dimensions—these create a sense of local citizenship. The groups, after all, are small enough that each knows he or she might make a difference to its flourishing. Through the course of a term, personal relationship can warm intelligence to higher degrees. Every so often, the occasion is so vivid and bright, so surprisingly alive with fresh ideas, so hilarious, and generous that it remains in the mind for years.

Yes, then, I do submit that in its better moments, the humanities seminar is an image of the good society. The seriousness bestowed on an interesting topic, the unseriousness allowed to flare, and most important, the equilibrium sometimes achieved between the curious, keen aspiration of individuals and their awareness of common venture: this is a citizenship in its own right.

Notes

1. Robert Venturi, Denise Scott Brown, and Steven Izenour, *Learning from Las Vegas* (Cambridge: MIT Press, 1972).
2. *Financial Times*, October 7, 2014, https://www.ft.com/content/a0b4cb1c-283c-11e4-9ea9-00144feabdc0#axzz3FZJuRadE, accessed May 17, 2017.
3. Henry Mayhew and George Cruikshank, 1851 *or, The Adventures of Mr. and Mrs. Sandboys and Family, Who Came Up to London to Enjoy Themselves, and to See the Great Exhibition* (London: David Bogue, 1851), 144.
4. Charles Dickens, "Please to Leave Your Umbrella," *Household Words*, 17, 423 (May 1, 1858): 458.
5. Ibid., 458.
6. Ibid., 457.
7. Thomas Hardy, "In the British Museum," *The Complete Poetical Works of Thomas Hardy*, ed. Samuel Hynes (Oxford: Oxford University Press, 1982), 98–9.
8. Simon Knell, "Altered Values: Searching for a New Collecting," *Museums and the Future of Collecting*, 2nd edn (Aldershot: Ashgate, 2004).

9. Neil MacGregor, "Scholarship and the Public," in G. Kavanagh, ed., *Museum Provision and Professionalism* (London and New York: Routledge, 1994), 245.

10. Ibid., 246.

11. Ibid., 246.

12. Ibid., 245.

13. Ibid., 246.

14. Ibid., 247.

15. Sandra H. Dudley, "Encountering a Chinese Horse," in *Museum Objects: Experiencing the Properties of Things* (London and New York: Routledge, 2012), 3.

16. Ibid., 3.

17. Ernst van de Wetering, "The Surface of Objects and Museum Style," in Dudley, *Museum Objects*, 106.

18. Julie Marcus, "Towards an Erotics of the Museum," in Dudley, *Museum Objects*, 11.

19. Benjamin, "The Work of Art," 221.

20. Dudley, "Encountering a Chinese Horse," 1–14.

21. Adam Bencard, "Presence in the Museum: On Metonymies, Discontinuity and History without Stories," *Museum & Society*, 12, 1 (March 2014): 29.

22. Ibid., 29.

23. Quoted ibid., 30.

24. Susan Pearce, "Collections and Collecting," in Simon Knell, ed., *Museums and the Future of Collecting*, 2nd edn (Aldershot: Ashgate, 2004) 49.

25. http://www.bing.com/videos/search?q=Antiques+Roadshow+UK%2c+28+September+2008&view=detail&mid=DEB29A247241443F7AE8DEB29A247241443F7AE8&FORM=VIRE, accessed May 17, 2017.

26. Pearce, "Collections and Collecting," 51.

27. http://www.standard.co.uk/comment/comment/religion-can-trump-capitalism-among-the-world-s-downtrodden-a3363666.html, accessed May 17, 2017.

28. Ibid.

29. Ibid.

Conclusion

Many who move through universities, and many who don't move at all, are ambitious for change on the large or small scale. Some make it happen. But whether you pass successfully from the seminar room to the surrounding world, or remain merely hopeful or deeply frustrated, as long as you are still there, the campus is the nearest universe. It's a mixed world, mixed and stained. Change *it*—not only, but early. The planet's universities, it says here, make a discontinuous multitude, and because they are a multitude, it matters how they are. Only to contemplate how many live in their midst at this moment now is to summon a presence which, whatever else it thinks about, should also think about the world it too often makes without thinking.

For all the imperfections of the humanities within the imperfect university, they offer a durable image of many-dimensioned life. They are worth improving on their own terms, but also because, just often enough, they constitute an exemplary microworld, whose success in balancing self and society could become a conscious offering. Every discipline can point to monumental achievement in the last century; no serious argument can deny the wide continuing contributions of humane knowledge. Now in the new millennium that distinction stands alongside the prospering of the everyday humanities. All the manifestations presented here have had their flowering in the last generation, when new technologies have dramatically extended old propensities.

In the first part of her immense little book of social critique, *Three Guineas*, Virginia Woolf asks whether she ought to make a gift—send a guinea—to support the rebuilding of a woman's college. Writing at a moment of world emergency in 1937, she builds a wide frame for her question: how to prevent war,—more particularly, how to prevent war by changing the aims of academic life. So, as she ponders the request for money in *Three Guineas*, she decides to place a condition on her gift, insisting—to her imaginary interlocutor—that "you must consider very carefully before you begin to rebuild your college what is the aim of education, what kind of society, what kind of human being it should seek to produce."[1]

If education is to prevent war, we must change our idea of the institutions that provide it. From this kernel thought, Woolf launches an openly utopian meditation as an instrument of critique, disdain, and hope. Her audacity is to recall founding principles and to picture the college, at pith and core, as something simple, inexpensive, new, and poor:

> it is clear that you must rebuild your college differently. It is young and poor; let it therefore take advantage of those qualities and be founded on poverty and youth.[2]
>
> The poor college must teach only the arts that can be taught cheaply and practised by poor people; such as medicine, mathematics, music, painting and literature. It should teach the arts of human intercourse; the art of understanding other people's lives and minds, and the little arts of talk, of dress, of cookery that are allied with them. The aim of the new college, the cheap college, should be not to segregate and specialize, but to combine. It should explore the ways in which mind and body can be made to cooperate; discover what new combinations make good wholes in human life.[3]

The words will seem, more than quaint, fully obsolete in the age of the research university, the corporate university, the mass-educating university. But Woolf was not writing policy but critical hope. She was thinking to the roots of "higher" education, embarrassing complexity by summoning simplicity. That last fluent phrase—"what new combinations make good wholes in human life"—recalls some of her earliest formulations of an experimental modernism, articulated just after World War I in essays such as "Modern Novels" and "Mr. Bennett and Mrs. Brown," where the task was precisely to reimagine relations between mind and body, by combining elements into new wholes. Now, twenty years later, with the near approach to a second global war, Woolf turns from theory of the novel to a theory of the university. The two projects—the modernism and the educational utopianism—are committed to motives as strong as the calculus of profit and loss, as strong but quite different:

> People who love learning for itself would gladly come [to the college]. Musicians, painters, writers, would teach there, because they would learn. What could be of greater help to a writer than to discuss the art of writing with people who were thinking not of examinations or degrees or of what honour or profit they could make literature give them but of the art itself?[4]

The picture is, after all, "interdisciplinary," and in the manner in which I find my students first intuitively understand the term: interdisciplinary as not only a meeting of academic fields, but as a crossing between creative and critical work. In 1937, the vision of interconnectedness opens outward to an image unembarrassed by its splendor. She envisions a college "where society was free":

> not parcelled out into the miserable distinctions of rich and poor, of clever and stupid; but where all the different degrees and kinds of mind, body, and soul merit co-operated. Let us then found this new college; this poor college; in which learning is sought for itself; where advertisement is abolished; and there are no degrees; and lectures are not given, and sermons are not preached, and the old poisoned vanities and parades which breed competition and jealousy...[5]

In confronting words and tones like these, too often overlooked in Woolf's corpus, we do well to notice our own wince and recoil. Wincing in the name of what? Realism? Sophistication? Irony? Anyone who turns from Woolf's words will be ignoring their continued presence, even when unuttered, in any serious reflection on the university and the role of the humanities within it. Every tart demand for efficiency, measurement, and output implicitly acknowledges the persistence of the "love of learning for itself," the vocation of free inquiry, the undead curiosity.

The startling moment is when Woolf breaks the glass of her utopianism, and admits she can think no further. The picture of the poor pure college meets the insistence of the Honorary Treasurer of the Rebuilding Fund: " 'What is the use of thinking how a college can be different...when it must be a place where students are taught to obtain appointments?' "[6]—leading a chastened Woolf to concede that here "was the 'reality' on which [the Treasurer's] eyes were fixed; students must be taught to earn their livings."[7] But the strange force of this concession is that the tone (keyed by single quotes) shows how nothing has been recanted at all. Opposing powers may be growing not weakening, but the prospect of uncorrupted shared inquiry is real, proven real because it recurs stubbornly.

It will surprise no one who has read this far to hear me say that Woolf's poor colleges have come to exist in those many sites of the everyday humanities. Here, if anywhere, Woolf's utopianism has found a place to settle, in all these free acts of knowing–being. They too are imperfect. But because they live outside the economy of money and status, running largely on curiosity alone, they don't stamp out easily. They don't need anyone's approval or endorsement.

A way forward, I'll say for the last time, is for the two estates—the academic and the everyday humanities—to see and feed one another. Let expertise become less mystifying, signified by experience more than credential, and let passionate amateurs make offerings that too busy professionals gratefully receive. Let them meet, and also let them go their separate ways. The university-based humanities, among much else and other, produce habits of reciprocity and exchange, individual insight and shared knowledge, extended in time and space. The everyday humanities fizz with the informality of ardor; they are not shy to affirm pleasure or to assign value; lacking the advantages of a self-conscious professionalism, they escape its constraints and caution.

Notes

1. Virginia Woolf, *Three Guineas*, in *A Room of One's Own* and *Three Guineas* (Oxford: Oxford: Oxford University Press, 2008), 198.
2. Ibid., 199.
3. Ibid., 199–200.
4. Ibid., 200.
5. Ibid., 201.
6. Ibid., 201.
7. Ibid., 202.

Bibliography

Armitage, David, and Jo Gudi, "*The History Manifesto*: A Reply to Deborah Cohen and Peter Mandler," *American Historical Review*, 120, 2 (April 2015): 543–54.

Bencard, Adam, "Presence in the Museum: On Metonymies, Discontinuity and History without Stories," *Museum and Society*, 12, 1 (March 2014): 29–43.

Bender, Thomas, "Expanding the Domain of History," in Chris M. Golde and George E. Walker, eds., *Envisioning the Future of Doctoral Education: Preparing Stewards of the Discipline* (San Francisco: Jossey-Bass, 2006): 295–310.

Bender, Thomas, Phillip F. Katz, and Colin A. Palmer, *The Education of Historians for the Twenty-first Century* (Urbana, IL: University of Illinois Press, 2004).

Benjamin, Walter, "The Work of Art in the Age of Mechanical Reproduction," in *Illuminations*, tr. Harry Zohn, ed. Hannah Arendt (New York: Schocken Books, 1968): 217–50.

Boix Mansilla, Veronica, "Assessing Expert Interdisciplinary Work at the Frontier: An Empirical Exploration," *Research Evaluation*, 15, 1 (April 2006): 17–29.

Borges, Jorge Luis, "The Secret Miracle" in *Ficciones* (New York: Grove Press, 1962): 143–50.

Boswell, James, *The Life of Samuel Johnson*, ed. George Birkbeck Hill (New York: Bigelow, Brown, 1921).

Burckhardt, Jacob, *The Civilization of the Renaissance in Italy*, vol. 1, tr. S. G. C. Middlemore (London: Macmillan and Co., 1904).

Burton, Robert, *The Anatomy of Melancholy* (New York: New York Review of Books, 2001).

Cohen, Deborah, and Peter Mandler, "*The History Manifesto:* A Critique," *American Historical Review*, 120, 2 (April 2015): 530–42.

Cole, Simon, A., "Where the Rubber Meets the Road: Thinking about Expert Evidence as Expert Testimony," *Villanova Law Review*, 52, 763 (2007): 803–42.

Collini, Stefan, *What Are Universities For?* (London: Penguin, 2012).

Collins, Harry, and Robert Evans, *Rethinking Expertise* (Chicago: The University of Chicago Press, 2007).

Conrad, Joseph, *The Mirror of the Sea* (New York and London: Harper & Brothers, 1906).

Conrad, Joseph, *A Personal Record* (New York and London: Harper & Brothers, 1912).

Damrosch, David, "Vectors of Change," in Chris M. Golde and George E. Walker, eds., *Envisioning the Future of Doctoral Education: Preparing Stewards of the Discipline* (San Francisco: Jossey-Bass, 2006): 34–45.

Daubert v. Merrell Dow Pharmaceuticals Inc. 509 U.S. 579 (1993).

Davison, Graeme, "Ancestors: The Broken Lineage of Family History," in *The Use and Abuse of Australian History* (St. Leonard's: Allen & Unwin, 2000): 80–109.

Davison, Graeme, *Lost Relations: Fortunes of My Family in Australia's Golden Age* (Sydney: Allen & Unwin, 2015).

Dewey, John, Review of *Public Opinion*, *The New Republic*, May 3, 1922, 286–8.

Dewey, John, *The Later Works of John Dewey, 1925–1953*, vol. 2, ed. J. A. Boydston (Carbondale, IL: Southern Illinois Press, 1969–90).

Dickens, Charles, "Please to Leave Your Umbrella," *Household Words*, 17, 423 (May 1858): 458.

Dudley, Sandra H., "Encountering a Chinese Horse," in *Museum Objects: Experiencing the Properties of Things* (London and New York: Routledge, 2012): 1–14.

Edmond, Gary, "*Supersizing Daubert: Science for Litigation* and Its Implications for Legal Practice and Scientific Research," *Villanova Law Review* 52, 763 (2007): 857–924.

Eliot, George, *Middlemarch*, ed. David Carroll (Oxford: Oxford University Press, 1988).

Eliot, T. S., *The Sacred Wood: Essays on Poetry and Criticism* (New York: Alfred A. Knopf, 1921).

Ericsson, K. Anders, and Jacqui Smith, *Toward a General Theory of Expertise: Prospects and Limits* (Cambridge: Cambridge University Press, 1991).

Evans, Tanya, "Secrets and Lies: The Radical Potential of Family History," *History Workshop Journal*, 71, 1 (2011): 49–73.

Foucault, Michel, "What is an Author?," *Language, Counter-Memory, Practice: Selected Essays and Interviews*, ed. Donald F. Bouchard (Ithaca, NY: Cornell University Press, 1977): 113–38.

Fowler, Karen Joy, *Jane Austen Book Club* (New York: G. P. Putnam's Sons, 2004).

Freud, Sigmund, "Family Romances," in *The Standard Edition of the Complete Psychological Works of Sigmund Freud*, vol. IX (1906–8): "Jensen's 'Gradiva' and Other Works" (London: Hogarth Press, 1959): 235–42.

Gates, Jr., Henry Louis, *Finding Your Roots* (Chapel Hill, NC: University of North Carolina Press, 2014).

Giddens, Anthony, "Living in a Post-Traditional Society," in Ulrich Beck, Anthony Giddens, and Scott Lash, eds., *Reflexive Modernization: Politics, Tradition and Aesthetics in the Modern Social Order* (Stanford, CA: Stanford University Press, 1994): 56–107.

Giles, Jim, "Internet Encyclopedias Go Head to Head," *Nature*, 438 (December 2005): 900–1.

Golde, Chris M., "Preparing Stewards of the Discipline," in Chris M. Golde and George E. Walker, eds., *Envisioning the Future of Doctoral Education: Preparing Stewards of the Discipline* (San Francisco: Jossey-Bass, 2006): 3–22.

Greenblatt, Stephen, *The Swerve: How the World Became Modern* (New York: Norton, 2011).

Greenstein, Shane, Yuan Gu, and Feng Zhu, *Ideological Segregation among Online Collaborators: Evidence from Wikipedians*, Harvard Business School Technology & Operations Mgt. Unit Working Paper No. 17–028.

Guldi, Jo, and David Armitage, *The History Manifesto* (Cambridge: Cambridge University Press, 2014).

Haley, Alex, *Roots: The Saga of an American Family* (New York: Vanguard Books, 2007).

Hand, Learned, "Historical and Practical Considerations Regarding Expert Testimony," *Harvard Law Review*, 15, 1 (May 1901): 40–58.

Hardy, Thomas, "In the British Museum," in *The Complete Poetical Works of Thomas Hardy*, ed. Samuel Hynes (Oxford: Oxford University Press, 1982): 98–9.

Heckscher, William S., "Erwin Panofsky: A Curriculum Vitae," in Irving Lavin, ed., *Three Essays on Style* (Cambridge, MA: MIT Press, 1995): 167–95.

Jasanoff, Sheila, "Research Subpoenas and the Sociology of Knowledge," *Law and Contemporary Problems*, 59, 3 (Summer 1996): 95–118.

Knell, Simon, "Altered Values: Searching for a New Collecting," in *Museums and the Future of Collecting*, 2nd edn (Aldershot: Ashgate, 2004): 1–46.

Kuhn, Thomas S., *The Structure of Scientific Revolutions*, 4th edn (Chicago: University of Chicago Press, 2012).

Lévi-Strauss, Claude, *The Savage Mind* (Chicago: University of Chicago Press, 1966).

Lippmann, Walter, *The Phantom Public* (New York: Harcourt, Brace and Company, 1925), 39.

Lippmann, Walter, *Public Opinion* (New York: Macmillan Company, 1941).

Louvel, Séverine, and Amy Jacobs, "Effects of Interdisciplinarity on Disciplines: A Study of Nanomedicine in France and California," *Revue française de sociologie* (English edn), 56, 1 (2015): 64–90.

MacGregor, Neil, "Scholarship and the Public," in G. Kavanagh, ed., *Museum Provision and Professionalism* (London and New York: Routledge, 1994): 244–7.

Marcus, Julie, "Towards an Erotics of the Museum," in Sandra H. Dudley, ed., *Museum Objects: Experiencing the Properties of Things* (London and New York: Routledge, 2012): 188–201.

Marcuse, Herbert, *Eros and Civilization: A Philosophical Inquiry into Freud* (Boston, MA: Beacon Press, 1955).

Mayhew, Henry, and George Cruikshank, *1851 or, The Adventures of Mr. and Mrs. Sandboys and Family, Who Came Up to London to Enjoy Themselves, and to See the Great Exhibition* (London: David Bogue, 1851).

Mnookin, Jennifer L., "Idealizing Science and Demonizing Experts: An Intellectual History of Expert Evidence," *Villanova Law Review*, 52, 763 (2007): 763–802.

Nagel, Thomas, *The View from Nowhere* (New York: Oxford University Press, 1986).

Nash, Catherine, " 'They're Family!': Cultural Genealogies of Relatedness in Popular Genealogy," in Sara Ahmed, ed., *Uprootings/Regroundings: Questions of Home and Migration* (New York, Oxford: Berg Publishers, 2003): 179–203.

Noy, Shiri, and Rashawn Ray, "Graduate Students' Perceptions of Their Advisors: Is There Systematic Disadvantage in Mentorship?" *Journal of Higher Education*, 83, 6 (November/December 2012): 876–914.

Pan, Lei, and Sophia Katrenko, *A Review of the UK's Interdisciplinary Research Using a Citation-Based Approach: Report to the UK HE Funding Bodies and MRC by Elsevier*, http://www.hefce.ac.uk/pubs/rereports/Year/2015/interdisc/Title,104883,en.html, accessed 5 June 2017.

Parker, Cornelia, *Magna Carta (An Embroidery)*, https://www.bl.uk/events/cornelia-parker-magna-carta-an-embroidery, accessed May 17, 2017.

Pearce, Susan, "Collections and Collecting," in Simon Knell, ed., *Museums and the Future of Collecting*, 2nd edn (Aldershot: Ashgate, 2004): 47–51.

Pinker, Steven, "Strangled by Roots," *New Republic*, August 6, 2007: 32–5.

Putnam, Hilary, "The Meaning of 'Meaning,'" in *Mind, Language and Reality*, Philosophical Papers, vol. 2 (Cambridge: Cambridge University Press, 1975): 215–71.

Quine, William Edward, "Transactions of the Illinois State Medical Society," in Edward J. Huth and T. Jock Murray, eds., *Medicine in Quotations*, 2nd edn (Philadelphia, PA: American College of Physicians, 2006): 249.

Reagle, Jr., Joseph Michael, *Good Faith Collboration: The Culture of Wikipedia* (Cambridge: MIT Press, 2010).

Robles, Gregorio, and Jesús M. González-Barahona, "A Comprehensive Study of Software Forks: Dates, Reasons and Outcomes," in Imed Hammouda, Björn Lundell, Tommi Mikkonen, and Walt Scacchi, eds., *Open Source Systems: Long-Term Sustainability. OSS 2012. IFIP Advances in Information and Communication Technology*, vol. 378. (Berlin and Heidelberg: Springer, 2012):1–13.

Sanger, Larry, "The Early History of Nupedia and Wikipedia.: A Memoir," http://features.slashdot.org/story/05/04/18/164213/the-early-history-of-nupedia-and-wikipedia-a-memoir, accessed May 17, 2017.

Sanger, Larry, "Why Wikipedia Must Jettison Its Elitism," http://larrysanger.org/2004/12/why-wikipedia-must-jettison-its-anti-elitism/, accessed May 17, 2017.

Sartre, Jean-Paul Sartre, *Search for a Method* (New York: Random House, 1963).

Sayer, Derek, *Rank Hypocrisies: The Insult of the REF* (London: Sage Publications, 2015).

Schudson, Michael, "The 'Lippmann-Dewey Debate' and the Invention of Walter Lippmann as an Anti-Democrat 1986–1996," *International Journal of Communication* 2 (2008): 1031–42.

Scriven, Michael, and Richard Paul, "A statement presented at the 8th Annual International Conference on Critical Thinking and Education Reform," http://www.criticalthinking.org/pages/critical-thinking-where-to-begin/796, accessed May 17, 2017.

Sharpe, R. A., "Art and Expertise," *Proceedings of the Aristotelian Society*, 85 (1985): 133–48.

Small, Helen, *The Value of the Humanities* (Oxford: Oxford University Press, 2013).

van de Wetering, Ernst, "The Surface of Objects and Museum Style," in Sandra H. Dudley, ed., *Museum Objects: Experiencing the Properties of Things* (London and New York: Routledge, 2012): 103–8.

Venturi, Robert, Denise Scott Brown, and Steven Izenour, *Learning from Las Vegas* (Cambridge: MIT Press, 1972).

Vespasiano da Bisticci, *Renaissance Princes, Popes, and Prelates*, tr. William George and Emily Waters (New York: Harper & Row, 1963).

Walker, George E., "The Questions in the Back of the Book," in Chris M. Golde and George E. Walker, eds., *Envisioning the Future of Doctoral Education: Preparing Stewards of the Discipline* (San Francisco: Jossey-Bass, 2006): 419–28.

Watson, Julia, "Ordering the Family: Genealogy as Autobiographical Pedigree," in *Getting a Life: Everyday Uses of Autobiography* (Minneapolis, MN: University of Minnesota Press, 1996): 297–326.

Whitehead, Alfred North, *Process and Reality*, ed. David Ray Griffin and Donald W. Sherburne (New York: The Free Press, 1978).

Wikipedia, https://en.wikipedia.org/wiki/Main_Page, accessed May 17, 2017.

Wilsdon, James, et al., *The Metric Tide: Report of the Independent Review of the Role of Metrics in Research Assessment and Management*. DOI: 10.13140/RG.2.1.4929.1363.

Wittgenstein, Ludwig, Preface, *Philosophical Investigations*, ed. G. E. M. Anscombe (Oxford: Blackwell, 1953): ix–x.

Wolf, Martin, "How to Share the World with True Believers in Global Terror," *Financial Times*, January 13, 2015, https://www.ft.com/content/bcccb5e0-9a87-11e4-86c2-00144feabdc0, accessed May 17, 2017.

Woolf, Virginia, *Three Guineas*, in *A Room of One's Own* and *Three Guineas* (Oxford: Oxford University Press, 2008).

Wynne, Brian, "Misunderstood Misunderstanding: Social Identities and Public Uptake of Science," *Public Understanding of Science*, 1, 3 (1992): 281–304.

Wynne, Brian, "May the Sheep Safely Graze? A Reflexive View of the Expert–Lay Knowledge Divide," in Scott Lash, Bronislaw Szerszynski, and Brian Wynne, eds., *Risk, Environment and Modernity: Towards a New Ecology* (London: Sage, 1996): 44–83.

Young, Robert, "The Naked Marx," *New Statesman*, 78 (7 November 1969): 666–7.

Zerubavel, Eviatar, *Ancestors and Relatives: Genealogy, Identity, and Community* (New York: Oxford University Press, 2012).

Zhao, Xiaoli, and M. J. Bishop, "Understanding and Supporting Online Communities of Practice: Lessons Learned from Wikipedia," *Educational Technology Research and Development*, 59, 5 (October 2011): 711–35.

Index